JOHN POWELL, S.J.

Fully HUMAN Fully ALIVE

A New Life through a New Vision

ThomasMore®
– An RCL Company –

Allen, Texas

Acknowledgments

Grateful acknowledgment is made to the authors and publishers for permission to reprint the following:

From *Escape from Freedom* by Erich Fromm. Copyright 1941, © 1969 by Erich Fromm. Reprinted by permission of Holt, Rinehart and Winston, Publishers.

From *Yes, World: A Mosaic of Meditation* by Mary Jean Irion. Copyright © 1970 by Mary Jean Irion. Published by Cambria Press, a division of Richard W. Baron Publishing Company.

Continued on page 147

Photo Credits

Dennis Full   148
Algimantas Kezys, S.J.   20, 46
Jean-Claude Lejeune   iv, 8, 34, 60, 78, 104, 130

Cover Design: Karen Malzeke-McDonald

Calligraphy: Bob Niles

Send all inquiries to:
Thomas More® Publishing
200 East Bethany Drive
Allen, Texas 75002–3804

Library of Congress Catalog Card Number: 76–41586

Printed in the United States of America

ISBN 0–88347–321–6

6 7 8 9 10   02 01 00 99 98

Contents

A matter of insight

"The Glory of God is a human being who is fully alive!"
Saint Irenaeus, second century

My brothers and sisters: I am sure that the most persistent and restless desire of my life is to be fully human and fully alive. On the other side of the coin, my deepest and most haunting fear is the possibility of wasting the glorious opportunity of life. My personal prayers vary according to the experience and needs of each day, but one prayer is never omitted: "Oh God, my Father, don't let me die without having really lived and really loved!" This is my hope and prayer for you, too. As much as I can be aware of my own motivation, the desire to see you live fully is the reason for this book. I have found something good, energizing, and life-giving, and I want to share it with you.

Over the course of my own life and in my quest for the full experience of human life, the most fulfilling and transforming moments have been moments of "insight." Sometimes these precious insights, which have widened the dimensions of my world and intensified my participation in life, have exploded like the Fourth of July. Sometimes they have come like the dawn, slowly and gradually bestowing a gift of light and life. I felt the joy of recognition and the warmth of kinship for Carl Jung, the great psychiatrist, when he added insight to the three traditional theological virtues; he said that the most meaningful moments of his own life were the moments of faith, hope, love, and *insight (Man in Search of a Soul)*.

It is necessary, of course, to test insights in the laboratory of life. Any knowledge that does not change the quality of life is sterile and of questionable value. On the other hand, if the quality and emotional patterns of life are changed, the change is usually traceable to some new insight or perception. This has been the story of my own life, and I am sure that it is the story of all human lives.

May I digress with a few personal examples? In my own adult life, among the insights that have profoundly changed me and my life, I would have to list the following:

1. Obnoxious qualities (lying, bragging, gossiping, temper tantrums, and so forth) in myself and in others are really cries of pain and appeals for help.

2. A good self-image is the most valuable psychological possession of a human being.

3. The success or failure of human relationships is determined primarily by success or failure at communication.

4. The full and free experience and expression of all our feelings is necessary for personal peace and meaningful relationships.

5. I am not personally responsible for solving the problems of others. Attempts to do this can only keep the other persons immature and train them to be dependent on me.

6. Love must be unconditional or it is a form of manipulation. Unconditional love is the only kind of love that affirms a human being and enables that person to grow.

These insights, along with many others, have been the subject matter of my previous books. I felt it was worthwhile to list some of these intuitions and realizations that have so deeply affected me, my life-style, and the dimensions of my world because the relationship between perceptions and life is the insight I want to share with you in this book. In one sentence: Our participation in the happiness of a full and human life is determined by our personal perception of reality. In the course of these pages I will often be calling this personalized perception of reality a "vision." As the saying goes, "What you see is what you get!"

Through the eyes of our minds you and I look out at reality (ourselves, other people, life, the world, and God). However, we see these things differently. Your vision of reality is not mine and, conversely, mine is not yours. Both of our visions are limited and inadequate, but not to the same extent. We have both misinterpreted and distorted reality, but in different ways. We have each seen something of the available truth and beauty to which the other has been blind. The main point is that it is the dimensions and clarity of this vision that determine the dimensions of our worlds and the quality of our lives. To the extent that we are blind or have distorted reality, our lives and our happiness have been diminished. Consequently, if we are to change—to grow—there must first be a change in this basic vision, or perception of reality.

It has been generally agreed that true and full human living is based on three components, like the legs of a tripod: intrapersonal dynamics, interpersonal relationships, and a frame of reference. In my previous attempts to write, I have been mostly concerned with the first two. My present concern is with the third: a frame of reference, a basic perception of reality through which we integrate, evaluate, and interpret new persons, events, and ideas. As a flexible person continues to integrate the "new," his or her basic perception or vision is itself changed. But it is always this vision, however modified, that controls the quality of and participation in human life.

This insight has made a great contribution not only to my life but also to my reflections on the human condition. I had come, in my own way, to the realization that love is the essential ingredient in a program of full human living and that love works if people are willing to work at it. I had come to see that communication is the lifeblood of love and that the experience and expression of emotions is the essential "stuff" of communication. I had also come to realize that no one can cause emotions in another but can only stimulate emotions that are already there waiting to be aroused.

After moving through these insights like milestones of understanding into ever new and exciting territory, I was left with a lingering question. Supposing a person were to act on all these insights, feeling perfectly free to experience and in a mature way to express his or her loneliness, fear, anger, and so forth. Where does the person go from here? Will the simple and open expression of these negative and burdensome emotions be sufficiently healing to change the patterns of his or her reactions? Fritz Perls and Gestalt therapists suggest that it will. Eric Berne and transactional analysts do not share this optimism. My own experience, with myself and with others, leads me to believe that a change in undesirable emotional patterns can come only with a change in thinking—with a change in one's perception of reality, or vision. This is also the contention of Albert Ellis and the practitioners of Rational Emotive Therapy.

It now seems obvious to me that our emotional reactions are not permanent parts of our makeup, the way we were in the beginning, are now, and ever shall be. Rather they grow out of the way we see ourselves, other people, life, the world, and God. Our perceptions become the habitual frame of reference within which we act and react. Our ideas and attitudes generate our emotional responses. Persistently negative emotions are an indication that there is a distortion or delusion in our thinking, an astigmatism in our vision.

For example, if I see myself as a worthless person, I can certainly anticipate many painful and persistent emotions—discouragement, depression, sadness, and maybe even suicidal feelings. But if I can be brought to realize, by the affirming and unconditional love of another, that I am really a decent and lovable person of considerable worth, this whole pattern of emotional reaction will be radically changed. As the distortion in my perception of myself is eliminated, I will be gradually transformed into a self-confident, assured, and happy person.

If I think of you as a friend and collaborator, my emotions on meeting you will be warm and positive. If I see you as an enemy and competitor, my emotions will be just the opposite. You will remember the little verse:

> Two men looked out from prison bars.
> One saw mud, one saw stars.

In the pursuit of the fullness of human life, everything depends on this frame of reference, this habitual outlook, this basic vision which I have of myself, others, life, the world, and God. What we see is what we get.

Consequently, if you or I are to change, to grow into persons who are more fully human and more fully alive, we shall certainly have to become aware of our vision and patiently work at redressing its imbalances and eliminating its distortions. All real and permanent growth must begin here. A shy person can be coaxed into assuming an air of confidence, but it will only be a mask—one mask replacing another. There can be no real change, no real growth in any of us until and unless our basic perception of reality, our vision, is changed.

A portrait of the fully alive human being

It would seem that the amount of destructiveness to be found in individuals is proportionate to the amount to which expansiveness of life is curtailed. By this we do not refer to individual frustrations of this or that instinctive desire but to the thwarting of the whole of life, the blockage of spontaneity of the growth and expression of man's sensuous, emotional, and intellectual capacities. Life has an inner dynamism of its own; it tends to grow, to be expressed, to be lived. It seems that if this tendency is thwarted the energy directed towards life undergoes a process of decomposition and changes into energies directed towards destruction. In other words: the drive for life and the drive for destruction are not mutually independent

factors but are in a reversed interdepend-
ence. The more the drive towards life is
thwarted, the stronger is the drive towards
destruction; the more life is realized, the
less is the strength of destructiveness. Destructiveness is the outcome of unlived life.

Erich Fromm, *Escape from Freedom*

Some time ago a friend told me of an occasion when, vaca-
tioning in the Bahamas, he saw a large and restless crowd
gathered on a pier. Upon investigation he discovered that
the object of all the attention was a young man making the
last-minute preparations for a solo journey around the
world in a homemade boat. Without exception everyone
on the pier was vocally pessimistic. All were actively volun-
teering to tell the ambitious sailor all the things that could
possibly go wrong. "The sun will broil you! . . . You won't
have enough food! . . . That boat of yours won't withstand
the waves in a storm! . . . You'll never make it!"

When my friend heard all these discouraging warnings
to the adventurous young man, he felt an irresistible desire
to offer some optimism and encouragement. As the little
craft began drifting away from the pier toward the horizon,
my friend went to the end of the pier, waving both arms
wildly like semaphores spelling confidence. He kept shout-
ing: "*Bon voyage!* You're really something! We're with you!
We're proud of you! Good luck, brother!"

Sometimes it seems to me that there are two kinds of
people. There are those who feel obligated to tell us all the
things that can go wrong as we set out over the uncharted
waters of our unique lives. "Wait till you get out into the

cold, cruel world, my friend. Take it from me." Then there are those who stand at the end of the pier, cheering us on, exuding a contagious confidence: *"Bon Voyage!"*

The history of psychology has been very heavily populated by learned people who have worked mainly with the sick, trying to discover what made them sick and warning the rest of us about the things that can go wrong. They have been well intentioned, and their good efforts have no doubt benefited all of us. However, an honored place in this history of psychology must certainly be awarded to the "father of humanistic psychology," the late Abraham Maslow. He did not concern himself primarily with the sick and the causes of sickness. He devoted most of his life and energies to a study of the healthy ("self-actualizing" people) and asked about the causes of health. Abe Maslow was definitely a *Bon Voyage* type. He was more concerned with what can go right than with what can go wrong, more anxious to lead us to the wellsprings of a full human life than to warn us about crippling injuries which we might sustain while trying to move along.

In the tradition of Maslow's humanistic psychology, I would like to begin now with a verbal portrait of people who are fully alive and offer some observations about what makes them healthy.

By way of a general description, fully alive people are those who are using all of their human faculties, powers, and talents. They are using them to the full. These individuals are fully functioning in their external and internal senses. They are comfortable with and open to the full experience and expression of all human emotions. Such people are vibrantly alive in mind, heart, and will. There is an instinctive fear in most of us, I think, to travel with our engines at full throttle. We prefer, for the sake of safety, to take life in small and dainty doses. The fully alive person travels with the confidence that if one is alive and fully functioning in all parts and powers, the result will be harmony, not chaos.

Fully alive human beings are alive in their external and internal *senses*. They see a beautiful world. They hear its music and poetry. They smell the fragrance of each new day and taste the deliciousness of every moment. Of course their senses are also insulted by ugliness and offended by odors. To be fully alive means to be open to the whole human experience. It is a struggle to climb a mountain, but the view from the top is magnificent. Fully alive individuals have activated imaginations and cultivated senses of humor. They are alive, too, in their *emotions*. They are able to experience the full gamut and galaxy of human feelings—wonder, awe, tenderness, compassion, both agony and ecstasy.

Fully alive people are also alive in their *minds*. They are very much aware of the wisdom in the statement of Socrates that "the unreflected life isn't worth living." Fully alive people are always thoughtful and reflective. They are capable of asking the right questions of life and flexible enough to let life question them. They will not live an unreflected life in an unexamined world. Most of all, perhaps, these people are alive in *will* and *heart*. They love much. They truly love and sincerely respect themselves. All love begins here and builds on this. Fully alive people are glad to be alive and to be who they are. In a delicate and sensitive way they also love others. Their general disposition toward all is one of concern and love. And there are individuals in their lives who are so dear to them that the happiness, success, and security of these loved ones are as real to them as their own. They are committed and faithful to those they love in this special way.

For such people life has the color of joy and the sound of celebration. Their lives are not a perennial funeral procession. Each tomorrow is a new opportunity which is eagerly anticipated. There is a reason to live and a reason to die. And when such people come to die, their hearts will be filled with gratitude for all that has been, for "the way we were," for a beautiful and full experience. A smile will spread throughout their whole being as their lives pass in review. And the world will always be a better place, a happier place, and a more human place because they lived and laughed and loved here.

The fullness of life must not be misrepresented as the proverbial "bowl of cherries." Fully alive people, precisely because they are fully alive, obviously experience failure as well as success. They are open to both pain and pleasure. They have many questions and some answers. They cry and they laugh. They dream and they hope. The only things that remain alien to their experience of life are passivity and apathy. They say a strong "yes" to life and a resounding "amen" to love. They feel the strong stings of growing—of going from the old into the new—but their sleeves are always rolled up, their minds are whirring, and their hearts are ablaze. They are always moving, growing, beings-in-process, creatures of continual evolution.

How does one get this way? How do we learn to join the dance and sing the songs of life in all of its fullness? It seems to me that the contemporary wisdom on this subject can be distilled and formulated into five essential steps to fuller living. These are normally taken in the order suggested, and each one builds upon the previous accomplishments. As will be obvious from a description of the steps, while each one builds on and grows out of the previous steps, none is ever fully and finally completed. Each will always remain an ideal to keep us reaching. In terms of a vision, or basic frame of reference, each of the five steps is essentially a new awareness or perception. The more deeply these perceptions are realized, the more one is enabled to find the fullness of life.

Briefly, and before discussing each, the five essential steps into the fullness of life are these: (1) to *accept* oneself, (2) to *be* oneself, (3) to *forget* oneself in loving, (4) to *believe,* (5) to *belong.* Obviously all growth begins with a joyful self-acceptance. Otherwise one is perpetually locked into an interior, painful, and endless civil war. However, the more we approve and accept ourselves, the more we are liberated from doubt about whether others will approve of and accept us. We are freed to be ourselves with confidence. But whether we are authentic or not, loving and living for oneself alone becomes a small and imprisoning world. We must learn to go out of ourselves into genuine love relationships. Of course the genuineness of these relationships will be directly dependent on one's ability to be authentic, to be himself or herself. Having been led out of self by love, one must then find a faith. Everyone must learn to believe in someone or something so deeply that life is charged with meaning and a sense of mission. And the more one dedicates oneself to this meaning and mission, the more such a person will develop a sense of profound and personal belonging and discover the reality of community. Let us now look at each of these steps more closely.

1. *To Accept Oneself.*   Fully alive people accept and love themselves as they are. They do not live for the promise of some tomorrow or the potential that may someday be revealed in them. They usually feel about themselves as they are the same warm and glad emotions that you and I feel when we meet someone whom we really like and admire. Fully alive people are sensitively aware of all that is good in themselves, from the little things, like the way they smile or walk, through the natural talents they have been given, to the virtues they have worked to cultivate. When these people find imperfections and limitations in themselves, they are compassionate. They try to understand, not to condemn themselves. "Beyond a wholesome discipline," *Desiderata* says, "be gentle with yourself." The wellsprings for the fullness of life rise from within a person. And, psychologically speaking, a joyful self-acceptance, a good self-image, and a sense of self-celebration are the bedrock beginning of the fountain that rises up into the fullness of life.

2. *To Be Oneself.* Fully alive people are liberated by their self-acceptance to be authentic and real. Only people who have joyfully accepted themselves can take all the risks and responsibilities of being themselves. "I gotta be me!" the song lyrics insist, but most of us get seduced into wearing masks and playing games. The old ego defense mechanisms are built up to protect us from further vulnerability. But they buffer us from reality and reduce our visibility. They diminish our capacity for living. Being ourselves has many implications. It means that we are free to have and to report our emotions, ideas, and preferences. Authentic individuals can think their own thoughts, make their own choices. They have risen above the nagging need for the approval of others. They do not sell out to anyone. Their feelings, thoughts, and choices are simply not for hire.

"To thine own self be true . . ." is their life principle and life-style.

3. *To Forget Oneself in Loving.* Having learned to accept and to be themselves, fully alive people proceed to master the art of forgetting themselves—the art of loving. They learn to go out of themselves in genuine caring and concern for others. The size of a person's world is the size of his or her heart. We can be at home in the world of reality only to the extent that we have learned to love it. Fully alive men and women escape from the dark and diminished world of egocentricity, which always has a population of one. They are filled with an empathy that enables them to feel deeply and spontaneously with others. Because they can enter into the feeling world of others—almost as if they were inside others or others were inside them—their world is greatly enlarged and their potential for human experience greatly enhanced. There are others so dear to them that they have personally experienced the "greater love than this" sense of commitment. They would protect their loved ones with their own lives.

Being a loving person is far different from being a so-called "do-gooder." Do-gooders merely use other people as opportunities for practicing their acts of virtue, of which they keep careful count. People who love learn to move the focus of their attention and concern from themselves out to others. They care deeply about others. The difference between do-gooders and people who love is the difference between a life which is an on-stage performance and a life which is an act of love. Real love cannot be successfully imitated. Our care and concern for others must be genuine, or our love means nothing. This much is certain: There is no learning to live without learning to love.

CHAPTER TWO

The statistics, the status quo, the speculation

Normal Day,
let me be aware of the treasure you are.
Let me learn from you,
love you, savor you, bless you,
before you depart.

Let me not pass you by
in quest of some rare
and perfect tomorrow.
Let me hold you while I may,
for it will not always be so.

One day I shall dig my fingers
into the earth,
or bury my face in the pillow,
or stretch myself taut,
or raise my hands to the sky,
and want more than all the world:
your return.

Mary Jean Irion,
Yes, World: A Mosaic of Meditation

The proposal being made in these pages is that one's vision, the way one interprets and evaluates reality, is the key to one's emotional and mental health. The theory is that our perceptions cause our emotions and affect our behavior. Consequently, we must begin with our thinking, with the way we are seeing things, with our vision. If we believe this, we will direct our personal growth efforts to becoming more aware of our vision and eliminating the faulty or distorted perceptions that have become a part of that vision.

Not everyone would agree with this theory or build an approach to mental and emotional health on this premise. In fact there are at least several other different theories about what makes people sick and what makes them well. And there are hundreds of different approaches to personal health and growth built on these basic theories. In this chapter I would like to locate my "new life through a new vision" approach in the context of contemporary problems and the current theorizing about those problems.

Unfortunately the vast majority of our human brothers and sisters do not look very much like the fully alive human being described in the last chapter. Abraham Maslow estimated that only one person in a hundred could be called self-actualizing or fully functioning. He felt that most of the others exist without really living. By common estimation most people realize only about 10 percent of their life potential. They see only 10 percent of the world's beauty and hear only 10 percent of the music and poetry of the universe. They are alive to only 10 percent of the deep and rich feelings possible to human beings. They stumble along the path of an unreflective life in an unexamined world. They survive with only a shriveled capacity for giving and receiving love.

Internal aches and pains tend to capture and hold hostage the attention of most people. They live "lives of quiet desperation," as Thoreau once said. The greater part of their energies is siphoned off by fears, angers, guilt feelings, hatreds, loneliness, and frustrations. They have little zest and even less strength to join the dance of life or sing its songs. "Getting high on life" is a meaningless cliché, a cruel hoax dangled before the hungry hearts of the naive.

Most people feel like tightrope walkers trying to keep their balance, afraid of the stress that can tip them into emotional or mental imbalance. Under any increase of social stress, the quiet desperation has for many flared up into acute and painful symptoms. A man loses his job and develops bleeding ulcers. A mother whose child dies goes into severe and prolonged depression. Actors, politicians, and others who live and perform in the fishbowl of public scrutiny often break down physically or psychologically. The protracted stress of the Vietnam War has left the American psyche strained and sour. The shadow of violence on the streets or in the home has darkened the minds and souls of most American city dwellers. There are so many sources of stress that make contemporary life a precarious adventure. Most people would be willing to settle for survival and safety.

You may know the statistics. There is something in us that rebels at and is reluctant to face them, so please be patient. One out of every ten Americans, according to the United States Institute of Mental Health, suffers from some kind of emotional or mental imbalance. One-half million Americans are in mental hospitals. Ten million Americans are classified "mentally ill," and more than 250,000 are admitted each day into mental hospitals for treatment. Two out of every three American hospital beds are occupied by mental patients. The most modest estimate of American suicides is 25,000 each year. However, it is commonly acknowledged that there are at least ten times that number of suicide attempts. Five percent of the adult American population is classified "alcoholic." There are people whose life-style is "characterized by intense and painful emotional isolation from family and friends accompanied by fear, distrust, guilt and shame," according to the Menninger Alcoholism Recovery Program. The second highest cause of infant mortality in this country is child abuse.

The fullness of life, the glorious opportunity of living and loving, means very little to most people. They have "had it" with life. Their hopes are dashed and their dreams are broken.

It is necessary to acknowledge that the emotional and mental problems of which we are speaking are classified as either "organic" or "functional." Organic disturbances are those that result from some deficiency in the physical organism, such as mongolism, retardation, and senility. Functional problems cover a wide spectrum, from the very serious to the very slight. The most serious form of the functional disturbance is "psychosis," a split or cleavage between the person and the real world. The most common mild form of functional problem or imbalance is called a "neurosis." The neurotic person is in touch with reality, but his or her ability to adjust to reality and function peacefully is diminished by emotional problems. The neurotic person usually has exaggerated reactions to certain persons, places, or things which may relate to job, family, or health.

If neurotic people cannot distinguish their emotional needs from physical hungers, they may turn into compulsive eaters. If they do not feel free to have and to express their emotions, they may well work them out destructively on their own bodies in consistently poor health, or they may displace these emotions on innocent bystanders. They may be perpetually edgy or have uncontrollable outbursts of temper or tears. All these, of course, are symptoms, not causes. Neurotic people are usually aware of their condition and the effects it has on others. Still, they feel quite powerless to do much about it.

The United Nations World Health Organization has singled out one type of imbalance as the world's greatest health problem: depression. The more severe form of this disturbance is called "deep depression" or "depressive psychosis." If this alternates with periods of exaltation, excitement, and intense activity, this up-and-down condition is usually called a "manic-depressive" state. Most people who suffer from depression experience feelings of loneliness and especially of helplessness and uselessness. Often they feel unworthy and guilt-ridden. When a person gets worn down by these emotions of depression and shows little interest in life and other people, he or she experiences what is commonly called a "nervous breakdown." More women suffer from depression than men, and the suicide rate among depressives is thirty-six times greater than among the general population.

The most serious and widespread form of mental illness is "schizophrenia." In the United States it is the main cause for hospitalization, and it is estimated that three out of every hundred Americans will be afflicted by some form of schizophrenia at some time in life, with the highest incidence coming between the ages of sixteen and thirty. The usual symptoms include withdrawal from all meaningful social life and retreat into an inner fantasy world. Schizophrenes are always deluded about reality and may hallucinate. There are marked and serious changes in sense perceptions, emotional reactions, and general behavior. People and objects assume strange appearances. Food and drink often taste very strange. Sounds come through as unbearably loud or scarcely audible. Internally the schizophrene often experiences depression, tension, and fatigue.

A paranoid schizophrenic person experiences delusions of grandeur, alternated with a sense of hostility and a feeling of being persecuted. But in general schizophrenes are more dangerous to themselves than to other people. The suicide rate among those so afflicted is twenty times greater than the normal rate. The general opinion is that one-third of all schizophrenes recover spontaneously, one-third remain as they are, and the other third experience progressive deterioration.

Because it is usually some form of social stress that precipitates these disturbances in those who seem predisposed, there have been many mass movements to places where there are no traffic problems, no demanding bosses, no pressures to produce, no regimenting clocks and calendars, few decisions, and no deadlines. Communal and country living have become very popular. Those who cannot physically get away attempt to escape by daydreaming a lot, getting drunk, or using other drugs. Some charter a perpetual flight into the future, living in the haven of a rosy tomorrow. Others find escape from stress in intellectualism—a world of books. Still others take on a perpetual frivolity, allowing any sin except "getting serious."

Of course, each individual's susceptibility to stress is different. Some individuals have a high tolerance for frustration and can take stress in large doses. There are even some who seem to thrive on tension and live on nerves. Others are more fragile and break apart quite easily. This lesser or greater susceptibility to stress obviously must be related to one's environment and biological heredity. The kind of home we live in, the chemistry of our bodies and brains, our diet and metabolism—all are factors that influence our ability to find the fullness of life. It would be a sizeable omission if this were not acknowledged. If a person is seriously troubled, there is immediate need for a competent diagnosis by a professional.

This has been a quick overview of the types of problems that cripple human beings and force them to forfeit the experience of life to the full. Now let us briefly turn to the methods of treatment that have been and are being used to help the troubled.

Even into our own day, treatment has been largely a matter of experimentation. Probably there is no one best way to help all people. Prior to the nineteenth century, physical cruelty and abuse were commonly accepted as the treatment of choice. Even the mentally ill King George III of England was subjected to beatings. Since the late nineteenth century, many theories have been proposed. Some of the theoreticians, like Freud and Adler, approached the emotional and mental disturbances of men and women through the minds of the sufferers. Others have been convinced that these disturbances originate in some bodily imbalance. Psychosurgery was once very popular, then fell into disrepute, and is now slowly regaining some of its lost popularity.

Another commonly used technique—based on the somatic, or bodily, approach—is "shock therapy." After induced convulsions, which scramble the brainwaves, many patients seemed to recover at least temporarily from painful emotional and mental disturbances. At first (in the 1930s) these convulsions were induced by injections of insulin. After ten years, other forms of shock therapy replaced insulin shock. The drug Metrazol was used for a while and was eventually replaced by electroshock (ECT), the application of electric currents to the brain. Today it is the practice to use ECT only after psychotherapy and chemotherapy (drugs) have been proven ineffective. Shock treatments usually effect some remission of symptoms. They obviously cannot reach the basic psychological disturbance. Consequently, there is a high rate of relapse among patients who undergo ECT without further psychotherapy.

Many recently discovered drugs, such as the antidepressants, have given welcome relief to many patients. But drugs, like ECT, can only be a crutch. Conceivably they could delay rather than hasten recovery since they alleviate the symptoms without touching the cause.

Another avenue of approach and experimentation is the so-called "orthomolecular psychiatry" of Dr. Linus Pauling. Pauling bases his theory on the fact that the proper functioning of the brain requires the presence in the brain of certain diverse molecules. These substances reach the brain through the bloodstream. If the body fails to utilize properly the vitamins and minerals found in food because of some genetic defect, this can be compensated by massive doses of vitamins or diet adjustment. Many psychiatrists have reported dramatic improvement in their patients through this means, while others remain critical and unconvinced.

We have been reviewing some of the somatic approaches to mental health. They are based on the belief that we must work through the body to help the mind. Basically, however, suffering persons know that they need help with their *thinking*. Many have sought help through psychotherapy from a psychiatrist or clinical psychologist. The results, when studied statistically, are not very impressive. The number of sick people who improve or recover without this professional help is almost as great as the number of those who improve or recover with professional help. This is not intended to downgrade the psychotherapeutic professions. It is undeniable that many people have been helped, and the professionals are only to be praised for their intentions and efforts.

As we have said, there are many systems of psychotherapy, as opposed to the somatic approaches, and they are rapidly multiplying. However, there are four distinct and basic hypotheses from which most of these systems have been derived.

1. *The Misconception Hypothesis.* This is the basic assumption on which the reasoning of our "vision therapy" is based. It is called a "cognitive" approach to emotional and mental health because it supposes that cognition (the way we perceive reality) is at the basis of emotional reactions and behavior. It further supposes that when faulty or distorted perceptions are eliminated, a person will be enabled to function and live more fully. It presumes that fears, complexes, and generally negative emotions are all traceable to faulty ideas, distorted perceptions, and destructive attitudes. These misconceptions are distortions in our vision of reality. Chronologically, this is the oldest of the four major hypotheses, and is associated today with Albert Ellis and Rational Emotive Therapy.

2. *The Expression of Emotion Hypothesis.* The theory of this hypothesis is that the way to a fuller life is through the release of pent-up emotions. Sometimes there are marked changes in people after they are encouraged to act out their fears, rages, and so forth, in experimental situations. This ventilation seems to be only part of the picture. Probably more critical than the simple emotional catharsis is the new awareness of the person regarding his or her emotional repression and the severing of the tie between stimulus and emotional response. The person ventilating has probably been repressing emotions, reacting to the emotional stimuli in life with outward calm in deference to the expectations of others. In the act of ventilation he or she asserts the right to open expression of feelings and discovers that he or she is constitutionally capable of such expression. Today we associate this hypothesis with Fritz Perls's Gestalt Therapy, Casriel's Scream Therapy, and Janov's Primal Therapy.

3. *The Redistribution-of-Energy Hypothesis.* This is the theory of Freud and the classical psychoanalysts. The so-called psychic energies of a person can be concentrated in or controlled by the *id* (basic, blind desires) and the *superego* (censor or conscience). When this happens, the personality becomes unbalanced and there are symptoms of maladjustment. When the balance of energy is restored by the *ego* (the mediator between the id and reality), the way is then open to the fullness of life. The person is freed from his or her intellectual conflicts and consequently liberated from the need to hold unconscious drives in tight control. When this happens, the person can then use the released energy in dealing constructively with his or her environment.

4. *The Behavior-Change Hypothesis.* This hypothesis bypasses as relatively unimportant the historical sources and origins of crippling emotions and behavior, and moves directly to changing the behavior itself through conditioning. Observable behavior is definitely changed through systematic desensitization, modeling (doing something in front of the person to show how easy it is), and self-demonstration (asking and helping the person to do what he or she feels incapable of doing). Observable behavior is the only concern of the behaviorists. We associate this hypothesis with the names of Wolpe, Eysenck, Skinner, and Ullmann. We are also familiar with the behavioral techniques of Stampfl's Implosive Therapy (a procedure of desensitization by repeatedly imagining the situation in which there is an anxiety response) and Assertiveness Training.

Psychologist Victor Raimy in his book *Misunderstandings of the Self* gives an adequate and reasonably objective description of each of these hypotheses. More importantly, he illustrates that in each of the last three there is some inclusion and incorporation of the misconception hypothesis. For example, the open expression of emotions (number 2) effects a very real change in the person's concept of himself or herself. After acting out their anger, fears, or frustrations, people see that they can express these feelings without falling apart or being utterly rejected. This new awareness will obviously change people's visions of themselves, of their ability to express emotions, and of the readiness of others to accept their emotions. In the redistribution hypothesis (number 3), there is an evident effort on the part of the analyst to help patients "work through their illusions" and arrive at new insights. (See Karl Menninger, *Theory of Psychoanalytic Technique,* p. 38.)

In the behavior-change hypothesis (number 4), the very conditioning and desensitizing procedures are geared to and always result in the elimination of some misconception. This misconception may be about an object ("All dogs are dangerous") or an action ("I can't give a speech in public"). In either case the person must be brought to the insight that his or her previous fears were without foundation. In Assertiveness Training people are taught through role-playing or performing tasks of graded difficulty how to assert their own rights. The coaches in this type of training help underconfident people to see themselves as individuals with rights. They help their participants to see that these rights must be asserted if they are to have any meaning, and that seeing oneself as subordinate and deferential represents a distorted outlook. It is obvious that such a technique presumes and builds upon the misconception hypothesis.

This brings us back to the basic supposition of our vision therapy: All change in the quality of a person's life must grow out of a change in his or her vision of reality. There can be no real and permanent change unless this vision is changed. We are now ready to investigate this truth in greater detail.

The vision that shapes our lives

Unfortunately,
children are excellent observers
but bad interpreters.
They observe keenly what goes on
but do not always
draw the correct conclusions.

Most children who feel rejected
are not rejected,
but assume that they are
because their impressions
and interpretations of what they observe
are faulty.

We are trying to change goals,
concepts, and notions.
Only such changes
can bring about permanent improvement.

Psychiatrist Rudolf Dreikurs,
Contemporary Psychotherapies
(M. I. Stein, editor)

Every baby born into this world is a living question mark. The first question asked is about self: Who am I? The baby proceeds to discover physical reality: hands, feet, and so forth. There is the experience of wetness and hunger. Then comes the discovery of personal emotional reality: security, insecurity, the need for gratification and attention. Somewhere in the course of this ongoing awareness of self, the infant gradually discovers that he or she is not the whole of reality, that all other beings are not merely extensions of self. This initiates the startling discovery of *otherness*. Who are they? Some are warm; some are cold. Some can be manipulated by crying; others cannot.

The thing that all other people have in common for the baby is that they are there. They are a part of the world. He or she must learn to relate to them. Thus, from the first days of life, the infant must begin the work of interpreting and adjusting to reality. As the eyes of the small body start to draw physical reality into focus, the small mind begins its own work of understanding, interpreting, and evaluating. It is the beginning of a vision that will shape a human life.

The human body is instinctively adaptive. The pores close in cold weather. The pupils of the eyes contract in bright light. Certain interior organs can take over the function of others if those others are defective. So, as the baby grows up, he or she will develop a whole repertoire of psychologically adaptive reactions comparable to those of the body. As each new being in this world is perceived, some adjustment to it must be made. This process will eventually constitute the personalized interpretation of and adjustment to reality of a unique human being. Most parents claim to see the first emergence of a distinct personality in each of their children even during infancy. The perceptual patterns and adaptive reactions of each child within a family also have very different emotional colorations. It is very important to realize that the individual adjustment and emotional reactions are the result of a very personal perception and interpretation of inner and outer reality.

At all times in every life there is at least a tentative vision. It is a necessary result of the dynamism of the human mind. The senses pick up phenomenological data—sights, smells, tastes, sounds, and sensations of touch. These are transmitted to the mind, which immediately begins to process and evaluate this material. Like a computer, the mind interprets all the different impulses, first grasped by the senses, and organizes reality into intelligible perceptual patterns.

It is something like receiving one by one the pieces of a mosaic or a jigsaw puzzle. The mosaic is "reality." It does not come all at once in a neat box. It comes piece by piece in packages marked "days." Each day brings new pieces. Every new piece adds its own contribution of deeper understanding to the total picture of reality. We put the pieces together differently because each of us perceives reality in his or her own way. The qualities most needed for the construction of an adequate and accurate vision are *openness* and *flexibility*. The trap to be avoided is *rigidity*.

Rigid people cannot live comfortably with doubt. They need to complete their pictures in a hurry. So they put together only a few of the pieces in a small and tight pattern. These few pieces are all they need. More pieces would only confuse them. And that is the way it was in the beginning, is now, and ever shall be. To hear such people talk, they would appear to have more certainties than anyone else. On the other hand, flexible and open people keep accepting new pieces, rearranging them to modify their tentative patterns. They are always ready to review and revise. They appear to have fewer certainties than the rigid people, and their conclusions are always tentative.

To use another analogy, rigid people are like detectives who take the first scraps of evidence discovered and immediately come to a definite and unshakeable conclusion about the mystery they are trying to solve. If any new evidence is uncovered, they insist on bending it to fit their original, premature conclusions. Flexible and open people are contented with tentative judgments, which they keep revising as new evidence comes in. Instead of bending the facts to fit their conclusions, they keep revising their conclusions to accommodate all the known facts.

Rigid people live fixed and static lives in a small world. They keep their world small so they can handle it. Though they won't admit it, they are terribly afraid to attempt any more. If they should open to reality, it would certainly overwhelm them. Their computers would be jammed. This tunnel vision preserves them from doubt and confusion. On the other hand, flexible people are growing people who live in an ever-expanding world. They sanely acknowledge that change involves both danger and opportunity. They know they can get hurt by possible miscalculations, but they also know that nothing is ever final or irrevocable. If one continues to review and revise, there can be no final failure.

The fact is this: We all need a vision, whether it is prematurely fixed or in the process of constant revision. A vision is necessary because of the restless insistence of the mind to find answers to its questions and to organize reality into understandable patterns. A vision also gives us direction for behavior. It gives life predictability. My vision serves me as a frame of reference, a source of adjustment to reality. Because of my vision, whether it be large or small, tentative or fixed, I know how to act.

If my vision or perception of myself is that I am no good and that people will not like me, then at least I know what my options are. For example, I can play at being a loner or I can become so repulsive that people will leave me alone. Or I can take the offensive, which is proverbially the best defense. By causing some kind of trouble I can get at least "negative strokes."

If in my vision of reality I perceive others as evil or dishonest, I will know how to adjust to them. I will lock my doors at night, put zippers on my pockets, and confide in no one. Similarly, if I perceive life to be an ugly struggle in a valley of tears, I know how to act: Cop out! Get high on drugs, liquor, or daydreams. Come into contact with reality only when necessary or unavoidable.

In other words, we all have a vision because of the very nature of the mind and its instinct to interpret reality. There is also a special need for this vision because it gives life consistency and predictability. A vision enables us to know how to act. Without some kind of vision we would be psychologically blind, stumbling and groping through completely uncharted territory. We would soon be confused and fragmented.

This vision serves as an inner resource by which we can gauge appropriate responses to persons, places, and things. It also becomes the source of our emotional responses. As we have said, all our emotional patterns and reactions are based on our perceptions. It doesn't matter whether the perception is accurate or not, the emotional response will inevitably be proportionate to our perception. For example, let us imagine that a child leaves a toy rubber snake on the lawn. If I perceive it as a real snake, it doesn't matter whether it is real or not. My emotional reaction will follow my perception.

Emotions are always the result of a given perception and interpretation. However, emotional reactions to a given perception can have a profound effect on further perceptions and interpretations. Have you ever been alone in a large, remotely situated house? You hear a noise in the night which you cannot locate or explain. It may have been a shutter blown closed by the wind. From that point on, every creak and shadow becomes suspicious. It is a kind of vicious circle. A perception causes emotional reactions, and the emotional reactions color and distort further perceptions.

We can laugh when remembering the night in the lonely house. However, such vicious circles can be crippling when they involve us in prejudices against other human beings. One bad experience can distort our perceptions of whole classes of people. Also, one experience perceived as disastrous can prove very crippling. It can distort the perception of ourselves and the interpretation of our abilities. For example: "I could never become a teacher. I tried to teach a class once and made a fool of myself." Or, "Some years ago I took a flight in an airplane, and we had to make a crash landing. I could never go up again."

Thus far we have seen that this vision, which is a highly individualized interpretation of reality, results from the nature of the mind. As soon as we discover otherness in the form of other creatures to which we must somehow relate, we begin to make this interpretation and to construct a personal adjustment to reality. This vision gives life predictability and guides our behavior by indicating appropriate responses. Finally, this vision is the basis of emotional patterns that define us as happy or sad, courageous or afraid, affectionate or angry.

There is one other result of this vision, which has a great and pervasive influence on the quality of a human life. I would like to call this result a "basic question," or mindset. It consists of a disposition in advance, or anticipation. Some people are sure of eventual failure whenever they attempt anything. "Old arsenic lips! Everything I kiss falls over dead." Each of us eventually develops a habitual, individual attitude as we approach life: persons, events, specific situations, work, study, and play. The question each of us habitually asks is always an outgrowth of his or her vision, or frame of reference. Sample basic questions: (Is yours listed here?)

What do I have to fear?

How could I get hurt?

What do I have to do to meet the expectations of others?

How could things go wrong?

How could I be tricked or taken advantage of?

Will I have to make any decisions, meet any deadlines, or take any responsibility?

Will I look good or bad in the eyes of others?

How can this bring me attention?

What "strokes" (rewards) are in it for me?

Will I have to reveal myself?

There won't be any trouble, will there?

Of course, the basic question with which each of us approaches the various persons and situations of life is not applied in all situations with absolute universality. Most of us are capable of some variation. But the vision that shapes our personalities is a habitual outlook, and we are creatures of habit. Habit makes us repetitive. The natural, human tendency to unity and a unified approach leads us into habitual rhythms, cycles, and reactions. At any rate, the point is that the basic question, or mind-set, is a consequence of one's fundamental vision of reality.

The basic question of the fully alive person, I would suggest, is this: How can I *enjoy* this person, place, situation, or challenge? No suggestion of hedonism or self-centeredness is intended. Nor is there any intention of limiting the *joy* in *enjoy* to sensual pleasure or emotional satisfaction, though these would be included. The essential condition for true human satisfaction requires that we remain fully active in all of our parts and powers—senses, emotions, mind, will, and heart. I cannot indulge my senses or emotions at the expense of shutting down my mind or turning off my heart.

In the question, How can I enjoy this? there is implied a strong positive mental attitude, a spirit of creativity. This basic question is also multidimensional: How can I get and give the most? How can I grow through this and help someone else to grow? How can I most deeply "live" this experience? What are the opportunities for loving and being loved in this day, this encounter, this situation?

Fully alive people find enjoyment in what others regard as drudgery or duty. They don't *have* to; they *want* to. They are aware of the thorns but concentrate on the roses. Each day has a newness about it; it is never a carbon copy of yesterday. No person is today who he or she was yesterday. Since their vision is always tentative and open to modification, fully alive people eagerly await new insights. These insights will renew them and their vision of reality.

Caution! In describing fully alive people, their vision and basic questions, I feel a certain uneasiness. I don't want to seem to be describing an ideal that is essentially unrealistic. It is quite possible for some people to get drunk on the raw liquor of Pollyannish hopes. Everything is always "ginger peachy!" Life is always beautiful! Obviously such people have lost touch with reality. I know of a wealthy businessman who demands the answer "Great!" whenever he inquires, "How are you?" There are many pop-psychologists who tell us authoritatively that all we have to do is think positively and optimistically. We should ignore our failures and just streak along the primrose path. This will change everything! This is obvious and dangerous nonsense.

It is obvious nonsense because changing one's thoughts about reality can change one's attitudes toward the facts but it cannot change the facts themselves. There is still grief over the death of a dear one. Failure still stings, and being overlooked still saddens. Of course, fully alive people will feel "the slings and arrows of outrageous fortune." They will grow into deeper, more sensitive, and more compassionate individuals precisely because they have suffered; but they will suffer.

The danger in the "Keep smiling!" quackery is that such romanticism and glamorization always end in sad disillusion when reality intrudes. "You can do anything you want to. Where there's a will there's a way!" is true only in soap operas and pulp-magazine stories. Usually the person who gets hooked on dreams is eventually buried in bitter disappointment.

Also, I have the feeling that the enthusiasts can force the positive mental attitude kind of happiness on people whose basic vision is, in fact, negative and pessimistic. This is really quite cruel. It amounts to urging the person to put a smiling mask over his or her essential sadness.

What we have to do is work with our vision. We must become more and more aware of its contents, discover its distortions, and replace faulty perceptions with those that are true. The truth alone can make us free. This is not a simple matter. If a person has spent twenty years building up a specific interpretation of and adjustment to reality, he or she cannot be expected to change that vision in twenty minutes. It is not as simple as wearing a smile or an "I think positively!" button. There is no real growth until the basic vision is changed, and growing is a gradual procedure, often accompanied by growing pains.

The sources of our vision

From its earliest days,
the child had to learn
degrees of approach and withdrawal
toward everyone around him.
He had to learn whom he could touch,
in whose arms
comfort and warmth could be sought,
where distance was the safer course.

Margaret Mead,
"Sex and Society," in *The Catechist*

If we could compare a human being to a tree, we would find under ground level at least five major roots. These roots nourish and tend to shape the total development of the person. They include a person's biological inheritance (brain, nervous system, and so forth), physical diet, metabolism, social environment, and a unique structure of personality. All of these affect to a great extent the way people will perceive themselves and the world around them.

There is an undeniable, even if somewhat mysterious, interaction of body and mind. It is undeniable that mental and emotional states affect the health of the body. Anxiety can precipitate an attack of asthma. I am personally convinced that health is basically an inner attitude. However, there is no doubt that bodily conditions, conversely, can affect psychological states. Anemia or an imbalance in the chemistry of the brain can bring on depression. This depression of physical origin can consequently distort the way one perceives reality. In other words, our vision of ourselves and the world around us can be profoundly influenced by physical factors.

After making this acknowledgment, I must leave all discussion and diagnosis of these possibilities to the biochemists and the medical doctors who are qualified and competent. I am not. I must limit this present discussion of human visions and their origins to the psychological, environmental influences.

As infants—and later children—begin to discover and interpret reality, they are acquiring a vision that is largely shaped by parents and other family members. Children may distort some family messages, and their most impressionable stages may unfortunately coincide with darker days in the life of their families. They may not hear what others intended to say, or they may be most open to parents and others during periods when they are least apt to transmit a healthy outlook. However, for better or for worse, a child's first tentative vision will by and large be that of his or her parents and family.

Children will see themselves very much as their parents and other relatives have seen them. They will learn to fear the things that their parents fear, to love that which they love, to value whatever they value. This process of osmosis by which children absorb into themselves the parental vision of reality actually begins with intrauterine or prenatal experiences. The peace or turbulence of a mother while she is carrying her child is transmitted to the child through blood-chemistry changes and muscular contractions. The child records these messages in his or her developing brain cells and nervous system. The mother's tranquillity and her traumas become the child's. The mother is saying to her child through these bodily messages that the world is safe and peaceful or that it is dangerous and insecure. To some extent, at least, these messages will affect the child's evaluation of reality and the basic vision with which he or she will begin life.

We have already described the newborn as living question marks. From the very moment children receive the gift of life, they also begin to receive answers and evaluations. Along with these answers and evaluations an emotional coloration is supplied: "Living in this world is difficult; the appropriate response to life is depression." Or, "Life is an exciting adventure; the appropriate response is a sense of eagerness and exhilaration." Children are generally docile and ready to accept the evaluations and suggested emotional responses that their parents communicate to them.

Of course these perceptions, interpretations, and suggested emotional responses are not swallowed whole or all at once. Repetition is the mother of learning. The dynamics in the development of a vision are these: A child, in a definite human situation and in response to definite stimuli, thinks a certain thought, for example: "I have no worth of myself. My only worth is to please others." In successive, repeated situations of a similar nature, the child thinks this same thought, repeatedly perceiving the supposed fact of personal worthlessness and the need to please. The original perception is reinforced by each incident. After sufficient repetition, what was at first a thought and only a questionable fact becomes an attitude and a conviction.

When this happens, the original perception has become a part of the child's vision. His or her emotional responses and behavior will correspond to this habitual perception. The child will be sad and constantly seeking the approval of others. It is another example of the fact that we humans are creatures of habit. Our habits define us. Our thoughts crystallize into attitudes, and our attitudes coalesce into a habitual frame of reference, a way of looking at things, a vision.

Both in the transmission of messages and in the ways they are received, the combinations and variables are infinite. Consequently, people develop unique visions and act very differently. For example: Through coded or explicit parental messages children, rightly or wrongly, may perceive their worth to reside in causing no trouble, or in getting good grades, or in being quiet, or in looking nice, or in being brave, and so forth, *ad infinitum.* Whether children have heard the messages correctly or not, whatever they have heard will have a profound effect on their lives.

In terms of the fullness of life, these early perceptions are extremely important. If children perceive themselves to be affirmed by their parents for what they look like, succeed at, or avoid doing, they will be trapped into frustrating visions and lives. To the extent that they are loved unconditionally they will perceive in themselves real worth identified with their persons and not with appearances or accomplishments. If they perceive only conditional love, which will be withdrawn as soon as they stop fulfilling the imposed conditions, they will perceive themselves as worthless. They will feel "used." The emotional response to this conditional love will probably be a blend of anger, insecurity, and a strong need for approval.

We have said that a baby's first question concerns self: Who am I? The perceived answers to this question, and consequent perception of self, will be the most important of all the parts of the vision that is being formulated. If children are loved or perceive themselves to be loved for themselves, they will develop a good self-image and be on their way to fulfilling lives. If they are loved for what they look like or can do for others, they are on their way to diminished lives.

The second question of children is about others: Who are they? Parents will answer this question more by example than precept. Children watch and listen for answers. They watch the expressions on the faces of their parents and listen to the inflections of their voices as they talk to and about other people. Parental reactions are repeated; messages are reinforced; child thoughts become adult attitudes. Eventually they know: Other people are essentially good or bad, friendly or angry, trustworthy or suspicious, safe or dangerous. They feel secure in this knowledge. If you can't believe your parents, whom can you trust?

Again it should be noted that the combinations and variables are infinite. For example: "Our family and relatives are good; everyone else is suspect." Or, "All people are basically good and decent if they are treated well." Or, "Some people are all right, but it is a safe rule to test thoroughly before trusting." Or, "People will be good to you if you are good to them." Or, "Be sure to bring pan scales when you deal with other people; that way you can carefully measure what you are giving and what you are getting. You won't be a sucker."

The third category in the total vision that opens or closes a person to the fullness of life is life itself. The child asks: What is life for? Who is a success and who is a failure at life? What is the most important thing to do in and with life? What is a full and satisfying life? The answers received will become an integral part of the child's first vision and evaluation of reality. The child's first goals and ambitions will be drawn from this frame of reference.

The general attitudes and value systems of one's parents are deciphered from their actions as well as their lecturing, from their reactions of satisfaction and disappointment as well as their stated principles. Their example more than their words will carry an indelible message to the growing child about the nature and purposes of life. The life situation of the parents during these early formative years of a child is very important. It may be that the parents are generally well adjusted and possessed of reasonable goals and value systems. But it may also happen that financial reverses, health problems, or one of many possible traumas can tip them off balance for prolonged periods. The life messages transmitted to their children during these periods will probably be filled with distortions.

Possible messages about the nature and purposes of life (check one or more):

Life is exciting; it is a real adventure.

Life isn't easy; it is everyone for himself.

Life is to have things: your own home, enough money for an emergency, security for old age.

Life is to get ahead, to prove yourself, to make people respect you.

Success in life is judged by how popular you are—by how many people love you.

You are worth only what you are worth in God's eyes.

Success in life is spelled M-O-N-E-Y.

Be sure you own your own business. Don't ever work for anyone else.

You only go around once, so grab all you can while you can.

Life is for having good times.

It isn't whether you win or lose; it's how you play the game.

Get your own plot of land and build high fences around it.

If you've got your health, you'll be all right.

Education is what is important. They can take everything away from you except your mind.

Eventually the child will be graduated from the home and family situation, but the old parental messages will continue to play softly on the tape recorder of the brain: "Life is . . ." "Success is . . ." "The most important thing is . . ."

This first inherited vision has parts called *self, other people,* and *life.* There will also be transmitted an attitude toward the physical world in which we live. Blessed are the children who receive a life-giving, energizing vision of the universe. They will be taught to wonder, to be filled with curiosity, to admire. Their leisure will be filled with nature walks, stargazing, planting gardens, bird-watching, and collecting rocks or seashells. They will learn to care for their own pets, to distinguish species of flowers and trees as well as cloud formations.

Sad are the children of parents who have no time for such "nonsense." (Unfortunately, many parents know that summer has arrived only because someone has turned on an air conditioner.) Such people are preoccupied with grubbing out a living, with making ends meet, and with watching sports spectaculars on television. "Mabel, did you hear what the kid said? He wants a new pair of binoculars for bird-watching! That's really a good one! No kid of mine will ever be a bird-watcher." Children of such parents will begin life with a "deprived" outlook. They will be able to see only a dingy little world. They will hear only the sound of the air conditioner and the voice of the announcer, endlessly describing a game that some athletes are playing on a field somewhere . . . somewhere they aren't. They will smell only the odors of stale beer and pungent cigars.

Finally, in the last category of reality, the child will receive an inherited vision of *God*. Many people have differing thoughts about God, who he or she is, what he or she does, and so forth. I do not have any last or even late work on the subject. I would deal here only with one truth about God, which is an unquestionable part of all Jewish and Christian teaching: the love of God for us.

There are two ways that God can be presented. One is very healthy; it will affirm a child and invite him or her to live more fully. The other is unhealthy; it can only threaten a child and diminish his or her prospects for life. In this second, distorted (as it appears to me) version, God loves us only *conditionally*. He loves us if, and only if, we make ourselves pleasing to him by obeying all his laws. However, if we fail—in thought, word, or deed—he will immediately withdraw his love. We will feel at once the shadows of divine displeasure falling across our lives. If we fulfill the condition of perfect faithfulness, he will then love us. If not, he will certainly vomit us out of his heart. It is a pretty heavy load to lay on a young mind and heart. If children later reject belief in this God, they are certainly one step closer to the truth.

The truth of God, as I find it in Jewish-Christian teaching and personally believe it, is that God loves us *unconditionally*. He says through his prophet Isaiah, "I have loved you with an everlasting love! . . . If a mother should forget the child of her womb, I would never forget you. . . . I have carved your name on the palms of my hands so I would never forget you." Of course we can refuse God and reject his love. If you ever offered your love to someone who did not want it, you will know what this means. Such a rejection of God's love constitutes the reality of sin. However, God changelessly continues to offer us his changeless love. He is not diminished in any way by our rejection. His arms are always open to receive us.

The ideal of unconditional love was dramatized for me in a story recently related by a well-known psychologist. It seems that a troubled married couple consulted a counselor. The wife complained that her husband was loving only when she kept their house in perfect order. The man agreed that this was true, but maintained that he had the right to expect a house in perfect order when he returned from a hard day's work. The wife countered: "But I need to know that he loves me whether the house is clean or not, just to have the strength to clean the house." The counselor agreed with her.

Children should not be taught that they have to win, earn, or be worthy of love—either the love of God or the love of parents. Real love is a gift. Real love is unconditional. There is no fine print in the contract. There is no price of admission. Simply: "I love you!" (I have described this ideal of love at greater length in my book *The Secret of Staying in Love.*) The God I know would say to the person striving to earn or be worthy of his love: "You have it backwards. You are trying to change so that you can win my love. It just doesn't and cannot work that way. I have given you my love so that you can change. If you accept my love as a gift, it will enable you to grow. You need to know I love you whether you do your best or not so that you will have the strength to do your best."

At any rate, Margaret Mead is right: The child has to learn from his first teachers "degrees of approach and withdrawal . . . whom he can touch, in whose arms comfort and warmth can be sought, and where distance is the safer course." Children learn who they are and what they are worth, who other people are and what they are worth. Children learn to cherish life as a beautiful opportunity or to despise it as a drudgery. They discover that the world is wide and warm and beautiful, or they walk along with eyes cast down through an unexamined world. It is all a matter of the vision they inherit. This vision is certainly the most important legacy of a child's parents and first teachers.

Inevitably children will revise this inherited vision. Their own observations and experiences will to some extent contradict, enlarge, and modify the pictures that were drawn for them. We have said earlier that the key to revising and modifying one's first vision—the key to growth as a person—is openness and flexibility. We called rigidity the trap to be avoided. Obviously, the more open and flexible a person is or becomes, the more he or she will be able to change the inherited vision and eliminate the distortions that diminish capacity for the fullness of life.

The rub is that some message of flexibility or rigidity is also a part of one's inherited vision. Parents transmit a disposition to rigidity or flexibility depending on their own willingness to risk and revise. If they are open to the new evidence that daily living constantly presents to us, their children will perceive this as an appropriate response. However, if parents are unwilling to live with doubt and are consequently rigid, their children will probably see this as the safer course. They will, in the beginning at least, imitate their parents in these inflexible postures.

For example: If a little girl comes home in tears after a disagreement with a playmate, her father may bellow some rigid, categorical sentiment such as: "I told you that kid's no good! Her whole family is no good!" Or, "You can't get along with anyone. From now on just stay home!" Or, "Stay away from those Catholics (or Protestants or Jews or blacks or whites)!"

For the kind of person who says these things, "all the evidence is in" on all questions. He is the personification of rigidity, and rigidity is the formula for nongrowth. It is also contagious. Rigid parents tend to beget rigid children.

Fortunately, as we grow up, new influences and other messages come to us from significant other persons. There is a constant turnover of new evidence in our lives. Through these sources we can modify inherited tendencies to rigidity and inflexibility as well as the other distortions in our inherited visions. But it isn't easy. Just to be aware of one's vision is very difficult. We are so easily deluded by our own ego defense mechanisms. Each of us has to contend with the deceits of an illusory self, the person we would like others to see and accept. It is hard for most of us to distinguish this illusory self from a real but repressed self.

The most profound problem of change probably lies at an even deeper level. The vision I work with gives me certainty. It makes sense of life. It gives life predictability and gives me a basis for adjustment to reality. With my vision, for better or for worse, I can cope. Without it, where would I be? What would happen to me if I gave it up in search of a new vision? It is now time to discuss these important questions.

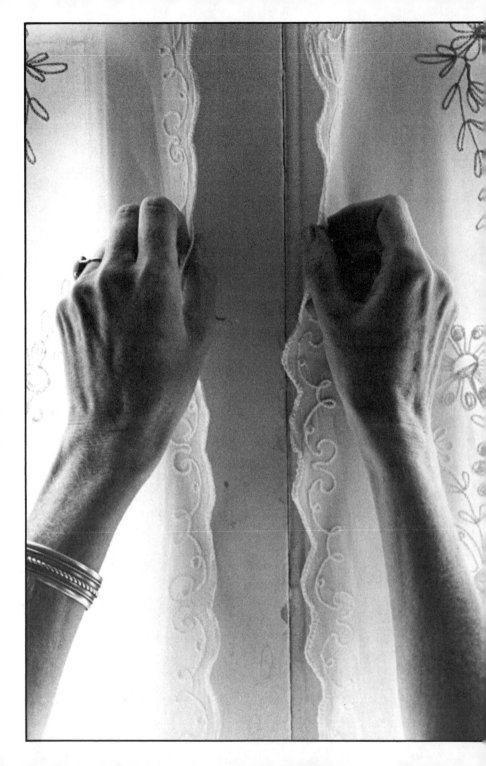

Persistence and awareness (of a vision)

Take stock of those around you and you will . . . hear them talk in precise terms about themselves and their surroundings, which would seem to point to them having ideas on the matter. But start to analyse those ideas and you will find that they hardly reflect in any way the reality to which they appear to refer, and if you go deeper you will discover that there is not even an attempt to adjust the ideas to this reality. Quite the contrary: through these notions the individual is trying to cut off any personal vision of reality, of his own very life. For life is at the start a chaos in which one is lost. The individual suspects this, but he is frightened at finding himself face to face with this terrible reality, and tries to cover it over with a curtain of fan-

tasy, where everything is clear. It does not
worry him that his "ideas" are not true,
he uses them as trenches for the defense
of his existence, as scarecrows to frighten
away reality.

José Ortega y Gasset,
The Revolt of the Masses

I would like at this point to investigate a very interesting
question. It concerns the persistence of our first, inherited
vision. Why does one's early vision tend to have such a
lasting influence throughout life? Are first impressions
really that lasting? It would seem that we would be eager
to give up the distortions that limit our happiness and diminish our possession of life. Of course some change is inevitable in everyone. It is the lack of profound changes
that is puzzling.

Let us imagine a man with a totally distorted vision.
He sees himself as a one-man slum. He regards other people
as mean and menacing. Life for him is an endurance contest,
the world is a snake pit, and God is little more than a cruel
illusion. Obviously such a man would want to stop the
world and get off. His perceptions punish him brutally.
Why doesn't such a person rethink and revise his vision?
He must notice that there are other people who are relatively happy. Some of the people who pass him on the street
are smiling or whistling. Did they swallow some secret of
joy? Are they high on something he hasn't found? What do
they know that he doesn't? If he were only willing to rethink
and revise his basic vision, he could turn self-contempt into
self-celebration. He could move from pessimism into optimism, from cynicism into trust. He could replace a negative

mental attitude with one that is positive. Why doesn't he? To a lesser or greater degree we all somehow resemble this poor man. Are we all masochists?

On the principle that if a thing is worth saying once it is probably worth saying twice, we have been repeating that the only possible way to grow and live more fully requires a change in our perceptions. A limiting, punishing vision is like a set of chains that keeps us bound. We are held fast in the same place, each day a carbon copy of the previous, and each year a repetition of last year's sadness. To understand why many of us remain voluntary prisoners of distorted visions, we must review briefly what a vision does for us. It may shed some light on why we are so reluctant to rethink and revise the vision with which we began the journey of life.

When we human beings first look inward at our own reality and outward at the rest of reality, we immediately begin looking for order, patterns, cycles. We learn to relate causes with their effects. We are looking for, in one word, *predictability*. Knowing what to expect gives us a sense of security. It enables us to make decisions about how to act. Soon our own actions and reactions fall into patterns which are based on our perceptions and adjustments to reality. Life becomes predictable, and our reactions take on *consistency*. We are usually willing to act well or badly to maintain this consistency. The opposite of predictability and consistency is *chaos*. Chaos implies unpredictability and inconsistency. Chaos boggles the mind and fragments the spirit. People who go through a period of chaos are often referred to as "disoriented." In their confusion, disoriented people have lost all sense of direction. Chaos is a very frightening experience.

And this is perhaps the main reason why we are so reluctant to change our vision, even when it is a cruelly imprisoning vision. There is a lingering fear that in giving up the old vision, which has provided predictability and consistency, I might fall into the chaos. I will be lost without a guide. For example, if I were to give up a poor self-image and learn to like myself, how would I act? What would happen? How would I relate to other people? If I were to give up my prejudice that others are basically dishonest and out to get me, how would I treat them? Would I have to start trusting others? Would I have to go so far as to reveal myself to others?

The trouble is that there are no guarantees that the new will be better than the old. Isn't it a question of one bird in the hand being better than two in the bush? Who wants to trade in a known for an unknown without some kind of reassurance? I know what I have; I am not sure what I will get or even what I stand to lose. In every change there is a death and a rebirth. Dying to the old and being born into the new is a frightening prospect. And there is always that terrible moment between death and rebirth when I will have nothing. If I give up the old vision, which made some sense of life and provided a source of direction for my behavior, will a new vision keep my life intact in the same way?

What we have been saying may sound like pure abstraction. I remember a personal experience that may help to illustrate more concretely the reality of this fear. A college girl came to me repeatedly in a counseling situation. For each visit she had a different problem. Finally, after working through very many problems, I asked her: "Do you think you will ever run out of problems? We must have hit the hundred mark by now." She looked down a bit sheepishly and said softly: "If I do, I won't be able to come and see you any more." The poor girl saw herself as completely inadequate in an adult social relationship. Because of her own self-perception she could not relate as one equal to another. The only way she could adjust to the reality of dealing with others was by playing a role of the "perpetually troubled little child."

Now let us suppose that someone were to say to this girl: "You see yourself as inadequate, and you have adjusted to this supposed inferiority by remaining a little girl. Now the fact of the matter is that you are not at all inadequate. You have fine gifts and you are a fine person. You must learn how to relate to others on a basis of equality, as one adult to another." What would be her reaction to this? Theoretically, she should want to believe in her adequacy and equality. However, she has based all her perceptions and adjustments on the supposition that she is inadequate and inferior. She has become comfortable and practiced in this role. A suggestion that she should change this faulty vision and begin acting in a radically different way would strike terror into her heart. She feels safe behind her fences and the face of helplessness. Consequently, she will tend to cling to her original orientation. Unfortunately, in doing so she has walled out a fuller and more human life.

A new example could be given for almost every person. All of us make definite evaluations of our human situation and develop definite ways of coping, of living within that situation. From that point on it is practice till functionally perfect. To revise the original evaluation would be like starting all over again and there would be no certainty of success. Consider the young man who has perceived himself as unlovable and has adapted to that supposed situation by becoming a professional introvert and loner. What if he were invited to revise his original judgments and leave his human hiding places, to come and join in the celebration of life? He would most probably cling to his vision and adaptation with white knuckles rather than risk the chaos of a conversion.

The famous psychiatrist of interpersonal relationships, Dr. Harry Stack Sullivan, in his book *The Psychiatric Interview*, calls these adjustments which result from a false or inadequate vision a "security operation." Once people have taken flight into such an operation, they have to fend off any new evidence that would threaten their original perceptions and subsequent adjustments. Dr. Sullivan calls this deliberate blindness "selective inattention." He attributes the security operation and consequent selective inattention to a desire to protect oneself, to stay safely within what we have called predictability and consistency. He says that this stubborn defense of a barricaded position "seriously reduces one's capacity to profit from experience." We have called this "rigidity."

Do you remember trying to pry something dangerous or undesirable from an infant's hand? Usually the little fist will tighten around its possession. The indicated psychological ploy is to dangle some attractive distraction before the child: a replacement. It works not only with the very young; we are all susceptible to a reasonable exchange. However, in this matter of revising one's perceptions and adjustments, it isn't like stepping out of one set of clothes into another. Our original perceptions, as we have said, had to be repeated until they crystallized into attitudes and were finally integrated into a vision. We are creatures of habit. We cannot step out of old habits into prefabricated new ones the way we change clothes. The changing of habits, by its very nature, has to be gradual.

However, staying in the old ruts isn't easy either. To persist in the old, diminished vision requires that one must constantly deny all contrary experience and information. One must stubbornly reassert his or her faulty vision in the face of mounting contradictory evidence. This can be strenuous and exhausting. It results over a period of time in considerable inner tension and stress. And the stronger the contrary evidence, the more energy the poor person must expend in the mechanism of denial.

This increased straining to deny, repress, and to keep our security operation intact means that we will be using more and more of our energy in this effort. We will have less and less energy for living, enjoying, and loving. While we may not acknowledge the explicit nature of this contest, we will note that anxiety and nervous symptoms, physical indisposition and fatigue, will become an almost habitual condition. We will become exhausted as a result of defending our imprisoning vision. Such an orientation to life must be labeled: *neurotic* (and painful!). The vision that the poor victim of rigidity tenaciously clings to for peace and security has become the source of considerable unhappiness and insecurity.

When people turn to a psychiatrist or psychologist, it is usually with the hope of an immediate relief. They want to feel better and they want a doctor who will be able to write out a psychological prescription which, when taken three times a day, will anesthetize all pain. If there is a need for "reconstructive psychotherapy," as opposed to "supportive psychotherapy," the result is usually the opposite. Supportive psychotherapy is designed to help a person get through brief periods that are traumatic or very difficult. Therapists help the client to ventilate pent-up emotions, to strengthen existing defenses. Therapists deal only at the conscious and symptomatic level. Their intention is exclusively to relieve temporary distress. Reconstructive psychotherapy, however, is usually needed by people whose symptoms are generally persistent and continual. The therapists attempt to deal, in this case, with the personality structure and the basic vision. When this is done, there is usually an initial period of disorientation or disintegration: chaos.

The person who is trying not merely to get by during a difficult period but to get out of a rutted existence and find the fullness of life will have to revise his or her basic vision. With or without professional help this is reconstructive psychotherapy. As we have been repeating: Our participation in the fullness of life is always proportionate to our vision. Whoever is not living fully is not seeing rightly. However, to give up an old vision in favor of a radically different perspective always involves the limbo of the in-between, the temporary experience of chaos. This is why there is always an initial period of disorientation or disintegration. It is a necessary part of the growth process.

Have you ever tried to cross a stream stepping from one rock to another? While perched on any one rock there is a sense of security. It is safe. Of course there is no movement, no progress, no satisfaction beyond safety. The challenge to move on—to step out to the next rock—is precarious and frightening precisely because of that moment when one is firmly footed on neither rock. The precarious and frightened feeling is comparable to what we feel at the moment an insight beckons and we are tempted to step out of rigidity into a new vision and into a new life. Just as it is foolish to want a dentist or doctor who can always cure us instantly without any discomfort, it is likewise foolish to think that human growth can be accomplished instantly and without pain. There is no painless entrance into a new and fully human life.

What is needed, whether it is accomplished with or without professional help, is a revised view of reality which will take into consideration and accommodate all previous experiences and all available evidence. The revisionist historian goes back and reinterprets, for example, the causes of a war long ended, with an objectivity which would have been impossible while the guns were blazing and the bombs exploding. In a similar manner, individuals who are seeking a new vision must go back, review the evidence of their life experiences, and revise the judgments, evaluations, and interpretations that have been controlling their emotions, their behavior, and their lives. No help is possible until they are willing to attempt this, and no change is real until they have done it.

Now let us turn to a different matter: becoming aware of my present vision. How do I bring my vision into consciousness for the sake of inspection? Before I can review and revise my perceptions, I have to be aware of them. Only then can I proceed to locate and modify the faulty perceptions that are distorting my vision.

The first requirement for finding one's vision and its distortions is a basic disposition of willingness to face the facts, whatever they be. It is a matter of courage and humility. This disposition of willingness will involve a specific willingness to say: "I was wrong." This is not easy for most of us. We are so much in need of approval and respect that we fear anything which might diminish our public image and sense of personal worth, such as admitting our delusions. In a larger dimension, we must be willing to admit a lesser or greater credibility gap between who we really are and who we pretend to be—between a *real* and an *illusory* self. Sometimes this illusory self fools other people. We come off as intelligent, competent, profound, or whatever our pretense is. Sometimes it even fools us. We repress into our subconscious minds the facts we cannot face, along with the fears, hungers, and angers we cannot admit. We stubbornly deny entrance to the truth which keeps knocking on our doors, asking for admittance and recognition. We are afraid to live and we are afraid to die. Ah yes, the first need is for courage and humility.

This willingness is really put to the test when it threatens to unravel a security operation and the consequent selective inattention. By necessity or choice most of us engage in some form of self-deception. We keep our egos afloat by some special ploy and block out of vision the rest of reality. In 1976 a tycoon, reputed to be the wealthiest man in the world, died. His name was J. Paul Getty and his fortune almost uncountable. When a book publisher asked him to write a complete autobiography, Getty unexpectedly agreed and soon sent to the publisher a single line: "J. Paul Getty became a billionaire!" He insisted that this one line was his complete autobiography. One line said it all. Among the legacy of his remembered quotations: "If you can count your money, you are not a billionaire." When reminded that "You can't take it with you!" Getty replied: "Yes, it would be too great a load, wouldn't it?"

I have no inclination to pass judgment on J. Paul Getty, Howard Hughes, or any other deceased billionaires. Human beings are far too complicated for such split-second psychoanalysis. I would simply suggest that if the words "He became a billionaire!" can really be taken literally as Getty's own summation of his total life, he did not live a very full life and he never had the experience of being fully human.

He may have been financially a billionaire, but if this one line really summarizes his life, he was personally bankrupt. Humans and human life are multidimensional. To live huddled in any corner of life, even if it is with an uncountable pile of money, is a life of serious deprivation. Poor Paul Getty. Poor us, if we settle for a security operation and the blindness of selective inattention.

Granted willingness, what then? I think that the next step is indicated in the suggestion of psychiatrist Viktor Frankl: "Let life question you." Dr. Frankl recommends this openness to be questioned by life as a means to find out who we are and what we love. He points out that most of us are forever questioning life: What will this day bring me? Who will love me? Will things go my way today? What will happen to me this year? How will this or that turn out? What has life done for me lately? Of course, no one can help wondering out loud in this way. But there is a deeper wisdom in reversing the process and letting life question us.

It is obvious to me that each new day—along with all the persons and events of that day—does in fact question us, if we will submit to the test. The needy, unattractive person asks me how much I can love. The death of a dear one asks me what I really believe about death and how profitably I can confront loss and loneliness. A beautiful day or a beautiful person asks me how capable I am of enjoyment. Solitude asks me if I really like myself and enjoy my own company. A good joke asks me if I have a sense of humor. A very different type person from a background very dissimilar to my own asks me if I am capable of empathy and understanding. Success and failure ask me to define my ideas of success and failure. Suffering asks me if I really believe I can grow through adversity. Negative criticism directed to me asks me about my sensitivities and self-confidence. The devotion and commitment of another to me asks me if I will let myself be loved.

Yes, every day does, in fact, question us. However, most answers do not pop out automatically, because we have quarantined them out of sight. Selective inattention has buried so many of my memories, thoughts, and emotions in graves of obscurity. My illusory self has served as a self-appointed censor, allowing me contact with thoughts and emotions that are judged to be acceptable, but not permitting me those thoughts and emotions that would threaten my fictitious identity.

Someone has humorously suggested that this repression and selective inattention are governed by three deceitful old witches: Shoulda—Woulda—Coulda. Instead of honestly facing my true thoughts, I am led to deny them by the conviction that I *should* think some other way. I substitute in my conscious awareness the way I should think for the way I do think. I convince myself that I do feel what I *would* like to feel. And what I *could* do becomes my preoccupation rather than addressing myself to what I actually do.

One helpful way to facilitate this process of being questioned by life is a self-analysis of one's emotions. The most fundamental supposition of this book is that our ideas (perceptions) cause our emotions. The patterns of our emotional lives are simple and tangible reflections of the patterns of our perceptual lives. Consequently, my first important effort must be a full, accurate, and conscious awareness of my emotions. I must have and acknowledge my emotions before they can guide me to the perceptions from which they have stemmed. Under every emotion is a definite perception. If I were to live in sensitive awareness of my emotions and be willing to dig for their roots, I would have easy access to the perceptions, to the vision that shapes my life.

I try to work at this in my own life and think of it as "vision therapy." Through emotional awareness and analysis I keep finding out very surprising things about myself and my basic vision. An example. Last summer I was happily driving along a busy Chicago expressway when the car I was using suddenly died. Right there in the middle lane, it died! I had the instinctive presence of mind to coast cautiously over to and through the right lane and onto the shoulder of the road. There was no thought of investigating the mechanical problem myself. The only thing about a car of which I am certain is its color. I did open the hood, but a brisk Chicago wind nearly blew it off. I shut the hood and tried opening the trunk with equally bad results. I knew that I was supposed to tie my handkerchief to the radio aerial, but the aerial of this car was built right into the windshield.

Finally I closed and locked everything and studied the terrain. On the shoulder side of the road, where I was standing, was a deep ravine and no signs of human life or civilization in it. In the other direction were six lanes of speeding traffic. I felt no inclination to try the ravine and an absolute aversion for trying a dash through expressway traffic. I did not know what to do. Finally it occurred to me to hitchhike. I tried to look worried, then pathetic, but no one stopped. In fact, no one even looked at me. I felt rejected. Don't they care?

After fifteen minutes a fine young college student pulled over and asked: "Can I help you?" No words have ever sounded sweeter. As we drove from the scene he told me of his interest in personal growth and I shared with him the mechanics of vision therapy. He asked: "Are you practicing it right now?" So we did it together. We decided that my emotion of the moment had to be called "panic." (I hate to admit it. My illusory self is competent, composed, cool, and always in command.)

In tracing my emotional panic to its perceptual source, I made a surprising discovery. Strangely, it was not danger to life or limb that was found at the roots of my panic. It was not the seeming indifference of the motorists who passed me by. Rather it was the fact that I was not in control of the situation, that I did not know what to do. Apparently I have always entertained the delusion that respectability is somehow forfeited by someone who is at a loss, confused, forced to fumble and improvise. Apparently a part of my own identity and sense of worth has somehow been attached to being in control of every situation. Once I discovered this, I was later able to relate this new awareness to other situations in my past life. By reinterpreting these past events I found that this new insight was strongly reinforced by old evidence. It was always there waiting for me to be ready and willing to recognize it. Being in control of, and knowing what to do immediately in, every situation was apparently part of my security operation. The elimination of this distortion is clearly one condition of my growth as a person and of my fuller participation in the adventure of living.

So the first two requirements for successful vision therapy are a willingness to revise one's interpretations and an openness to be questioned by life. A third requirement would be finding times for silence and solitude. We are all victims of too much noise, too many distractions—victims of what a well-known psychologist has called "stimulus flooding." To come into contact with one's vision, one has to practice some kind of active and sensitive listening to oneself. For such an in-depth effort, silence and solitude are indispensable. "The unreflected life," to requote Socrates, "isn't worth living." The kind of listening I am suggesting here is a peaceful review of the rhythms of one's recent life. It would include a recollection of recent events and one's personal response to those events. Through analysis of the emotional reactions, the perceptions under them will surface. These must be open to inspection and review and, to the extent needed, revision. We shall talk later about how these perceptions are permanently revised. This is the change of vision that alone can bring fuller participation in life. For now, however, we are interested only in locating or becoming aware of that vision. Silence, solitude, and reflection are very necessary to this effort.

An autobiographical illustration of all the above. Some years ago a close friend asked me: "Are you enjoying your life?" Life itself had been asking me that question but I wasn't listening. In answering my friend, I said: "I believe in what I am doing. I find it meaningful. I think I am helping others. I . . . well, no, I don't think I am really enjoying my life." The insight of my answer surprised me. I had been thinking only in terms of commitment, meaningfulness, and service. Strangely, I had not been thinking in terms of personal enjoyment. I began taking my friend's question and my answer into the think tanks of silence and solitude. There it became clear to me that even if a person is doing a fine thing for pure motives, if he or she is not enjoying it, something is wrong. No one should be deprived of joy in one's life and work.

Wanting to understand why I seemed to be experiencing more struggle than joy, I tried to get in touch with the emotional patterns of my life. It was immediately evident that frustration and anger were too dominant in those patterns. Without retelling the dramatic story of my life and how I miraculously came to be saved by startling insights, I must tell you that I did find two faulty perceptions or distortions in my total vision. I think that they were largely responsible for the frustration and anger which I was experiencing at that time. As these distortions have been more and more eliminated I have noticed a proportionate diminution of those negative emotions, and an increase of joy.

The distortions I found were these: (1) I saw myself as responsible for solving the problems of the many people who were coming to me for help. I was perceiving my value and identity as essentially connected with my ability to dictate instant solutions to tangled problems and bring immediate peace to all the sufferers. (2) I found in myself a strong, almost compulsive, need to please others—to meet their expectations. This delusion—that I had to be "for others" and never "for myself"—was truly a ring in my nose by which I was being led around. The discovery of this delusion led to a whole explosion of insights about the need to love oneself in balance with loving other people.

As I began acting on these insights, prompted by the question of a friend and found in solitude and reflection, I began to experience more and more of the joy that had been eluding me. Of course, one has to establish insights as permanent by acting on them. We must "do" the truth as well as believe it. We must continue to act on our lights or the light will fail. The old distortions and emotional syndromes die slowly because we are creatures of habit. New habits must be built from the ground up. However, the more one sees clearly the falseness or distortion of previous perceptions, the more one will be liberated from former tyrants, and will begin to enjoy the fullness of life.

There should be quiet times in every life for such reflection, reevaluation, and reinterpretation. It is also very profitable, if not necessary, to key into emotions—especially negative emotions—while they are being experienced. Memory tends to distort. These emotional reactions can be more accurately traced to perceptual roots and possible distortions if they are inspected while still on the vine.

Such are the requirements of vision therapy. When it has become a way of life, and one is alert to the signals of negative emotions as symptomatic of perceptual distortions, a fuller and more human life cannot be far away. We shall say more of vision therapy in the next two chapters. There we will take up some of the more common distortions found among humans and discuss in detail the mechanics of vision therapy.

Some common misconceptions

. . . the task of logotherapy is to reveal the flaws in improper logical grounds for a world-view and thereby to effect a readjustment of that view.

Psychiatrist Viktor Frankl,
The Doctor and the Soul

Most neurotic suffering results from an erroneous outlook. In one way or another the neurotic has acquired a picture of his place in life which simply isn't true. Feeling helpless in the midst of conflicting claims, he allows his life to be molded by circumstances until he feels himself to be little more than a victim of fate.

Can any therapy really serve its purpose if unrealistic views of life are left unchallenged? . . . Recognizing how an individual's vision is limited by his own life experience, Frankl perceives the therapeutic task as including the marshaling of arguments to challenge destructive world views.

Psychologist Robert Leslie,
Jesus and Logotherapy

In the last chapter suggestions were made for locating the vision that shapes our lives. Vision therapy, as recommended, is designed to help us find the misconceptions and distortions that lie at the roots of our unhappiness and neurotic suffering. To be successful practitioners of vision therapy we must first ask: What am I feeling? Only then can we move to the causes of our feelings and ask about the perceptions or ideas from which the feelings have resulted. How am I viewing this situation? What is there in my general outlook that this situation should produce these emotions?

To get to the distortions that fester like embedded slivers in the flesh of our emotions, some emotional clearance is usually necessary. After discharging painful emotions, verbally or nonverbally, we can usually think more clearly. Heavy emotions tend to bend the mind out of shape. This emotional clearance is like clearing the air or silencing a deafening noise. An overload of emotions almost always obscures one's vision beyond recognition. This problem is further complicated by what I would like to call a "lifelong buildup" of emotions. Undischarged emotions collect and have a cumulative effect. For example, let us suppose that people who have outranked me (parents, teachers, and the like) have repeatedly called me "stupid." At such times I could never discharge my hurt and anger because these detractors were my parents, had positions of authority over me and could punish me, or were bigger than I.

After years of such accumulation, I might be ripe and ready to overreact. I will probably report a very deep hurt or a furious anger at any suggestion that I have inferior intelligence. In other words, the next time someone calls me "stupid" my reaction will not be directed exclusively at that person. In a very real way my reactions will be directed to the hundreds of people who have, over the years, been in the "firing squad" which assassinated my intellectual self-confidence. I am really reacting to my parents, my teachers, my camp counselor, and the big kid down the block who picked on me.

One of the reasons, no doubt, that Gestalt Therapy has helped many people is that it has provided an acceptable means of ventilating, discharging, and thus defusing many years of emotional buildup. A good scream, a good cry, a good kick at the symbolic pillow, under carefully arranged circumstances in which no one else will get hurt or be manipulated, is probably a very good idea. Having a friend who provides the needed atmosphere for free emotional communication is an invaluable help to vision therapy and personal growth. Only when we exercise our right to have and to express our true feelings do we become capable of finding the vision that lies under those feelings and causes them. Emotions are always an outgrowth of perceptions.

In a book called *Outwitting Our Nerves* (2d edition), two doctors, Jackson and Salisbury, have worked out a cause-effect schematic diagram to illustrate how wrong ideas or misconceptions lie at the roots of unhappy living and social maladjustment. The diagram of the doctors indicates that all hope to restore a person to adjusted and joyful living lies in reversing the formula, in correcting wrong ideas or misconceptions.

Jackson-Salisbury *Diagram for Maladjusted and Unhappy Living*

Lack of adaptation to social environment
  caused by
Lack of harmony within the personality
  caused by
Inappropriate emotions
  caused by
Wrong ideas or ignorance

Working backward, the *cure* naturally would be:

Right ideas
  resulting in
Appropriate emotions
  resulting in
Harmony within the personality
  resulting in
Readjustment to the social environment

Obviously, "wrong ideas or ignorance" in the diagram corresponds to what we have been calling "misconceptions" or "distortions" in one's basic vision. The message is the same: *Health and wholeness begin in the head,* with healthy ideas, energizing attitudes, a vision of vitality. When perceptions get twisted, one's emotional life also gets twisted, and these discordant emotions cause disharmony in the total personality. At this point you've got trouble in River City.

Neurotics wear themselves out trying to cope with the civil war that is going on inside them. They can also be very wearing on others. If neurotics are helped to eliminate the misconceptions or distortions at the bottom of their struggles, this will effect an immediate improvement in their emotional patterns, which in turn will tend to harmonize the whole personality. Such people are then enabled to relate comfortably with others, to enjoy life.

Before our discussion of the misconceptions thought to be most prevalent among human beings, let's try an experiment. It is a homemade little test of one's vision. Relax now. You cannot flunk. Besides, the purpose of this test is primarily to help you become aware of the various dimensions embraced in your vision of reality. It may have some diagnostic value, but that is secondary, and you can decide for yourself its diagnostic validity.

We have already suggested that there are five main categories in the spectrum of a vision: self, other people, life, the world, God. Most students of human nature would probably agree that of these five categories the most important by far is the first: how you see yourself. All ability to love begins with and is conditioned by one's ability to love oneself. If we are to love others and to love life itself, we must have a true love for ourselves, a healthy self-image, a sense of self-appreciation. Consequently, the experts believe that the most harmful and crippling distortions in anyone's vision of reality are usually clustered in this area. Furthermore, the distortions in how we see other people, life, the world, and God are usually traceable to some distortion in the way we see ourselves. However, a check of all areas is in order.

Below you will find some fundamental either/or descriptions under each of the five suggested categories. On a separate sheet of paper, put the numbers from 1 to 100 in a vertical column. After each number draw a straight horizontal line, two or three inches in length. It is important that the lines be directly under one another for the sake of graphing to be done later. Above the first line put the letters A, B, C, D, and E spaced out across the width of the line, with the letter A at the far left and the letter E at the far right. If your answer (judgment, evaluation) verges more to the first of the two given alternatives, put a dot or an X on the line proportionately close to the left end of the line, under or between A or B. If your answer tends more toward the second alternative, indicate this by placing the dot or X proportionately close to the right end of the line, under or between D or E. If you see your answer falling in the middle, then put the dot or X under the C. Here is an example:

> 1. (I am) Good/Bad

    A   **B**   **C**   **D**   **E**

I put the X closer to the left end of the line, under the B, because I see myself as more good than bad. If I saw myself as completely good in every way, I would have put the X under the A. After you have prepared your answer sheet, consider the choices offered below and mark your answer sheet accordingly. Above all else be honest! Don't mark what you *should, would* or *could* think, but in every case what you actually *do* think.

> I. Who am I?
>
> > 1. Good/Bad
> >
> > 2. Compassionate/Unfeeling

3. Generous/Selfish

4. Responsible/Undependable

5. Hardworking/Lazy

6. Capable of personal decisions/Indecisive

7. Authentic/Phoney

8. Involved in social concerns/Uninvolved

9. Interested in others/Interested only in self

10. Loyal/Disloyal

11. Gifted/Ungifted

12. Superior to most others/Inferior

13. Intelligent/Unintelligent

14. Great in potential/Little potential

15. In control of life/Out of control of life

16. Good-looking/Ugly

17. Lovable/Unlovable

18. Many pleasing mannerisms/Few

19. Grateful/Ungrateful

20. Emotionally warm/Cold

21. Deep/Superficial

22. Interesting/Boring

23. Active/Passive

24. Consistent/Inconsistent

25. Independent/Overly dependent

26. Important to others/Unimportant

27. Needed/Not needed

28. Loved by many/Loved by few

29. Supported by many/Supported by few

30. My love wanted by many/Wanted by few

31. Valued highly by many/By few

32. Valued for self/For what I can give

33. Add much to group gatherings/Add little

34. Give much joy to others/Give little

35. Cooperative/Uncooperative

II. Who are other people?

36. Essentially good/Bad

37. Peaceful/Hostile

38. Trustworthy/Suspicious

39. Ready to help me/Disinterested in me

40. Loving/Selfish

41. Generous/Greedy

42. Concerned about others/Only about themselves

43. Honest/Dishonest

44. Compassionate/Unfeeling

45. Loyal/Disloyal

46. Grateful/Ungrateful

47. Similar to me/Unlike me

48. Responsible/Undependable

49. Emotionally warm/Cold

50. Lovable/Unlovable

51. Cooperative/Uncooperative

52. Collaborators/Competitors

53. Balanced/Unbalanced

54. Hurting and needy/In no pain and no need

55. Authentic/Phoney

III. What is life?

56. A pleasant experience/A struggle

57. Important/Doesn't really matter

58. Beautiful/Ugly

59. An adventure/An endurance contest

60. An education/A disillusionment

61. Satisfying/Dissatisfying

62. Challenging/Defeating

63. Meaningful/Meaningless

64. Too short/Too long

65. Exciting/Boring

66. A time for growing/For surviving

67. Perpetually changing and new/Sadly repetitious

68. A time for giving/A time for getting

69. I wouldn't miss it for anything/Sorry I got into it

70. Money is relatively unimportant/Almost everything

71. Tomorrows are eagerly awaited/Dreaded

72. Time is valuable/Worthless

73. Old age is a mellow time/A sad time

74. Suffering can be a time of growth/An evil to be avoided

75. Death is a beginning/A tragedy

IV. What is the physical world?

76. Nature is beautiful/Unimpressive

77. The physical world is important/Unimportant

78. The physical world is fascinating/Dull

79. I have great interest in geography-geology/No interest

80. Animal pets are very enjoyable/A nuisance

81. I enjoy gardens immensely/Never notice them

82. I have much interest in nature-related hobbies/No involvement

83. Solar system is mind-staggering/Is irrelevant to me

84. Archaeology excites great curiosity/Means nothing to me

85. Certain natural scenes are special to me/Have no significance

86. Ecology is a great concern/Excites no interest

87. The animal kingdom is interesting/Is irrelevant to me

88. Stars are breathtaking/Rarely notice them

89. Nature walks are delightful/Silly and boring

90. Seasons are beautiful/A bother

V. Who is God?

91. A father-mother/A tyrant-taskmaster

92. Unconditionally loving/Conditionally loving

93. Forgiving/Angry and unrelenting

94. Interested in me/Not at all interested

95. Near and close/Distant and detached

96. Reassuring/Frightening

97. Comforting/Upsetting

98. Warm/Cold

99. Understanding/Intolerant

100. Affirming/Threatening

After you have completed marking all 100 questions, draw a line after numbers 35 (self), 55 (other people), 75 (life), 90 (world), 100 (God). Then connect all the Xs or dots with straight lines. Your answer sheet should look something like this:

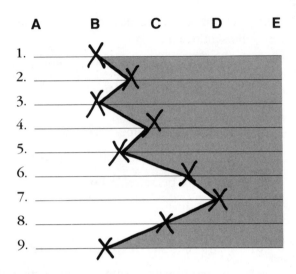

The part on the right side of the line which connects the Xs or dots may be filled in for graphic purposes (as in the illustration). Remember that the primary purpose of this test is not diagnosis but rather an awareness of the dimensions and aspects of a person's total vision. However, it is probably true that the larger the shaded area, the healthier and more human the vision of that person.

Please note well that this last statement is valid only up to a point. First of all, we are never so accurately in touch with our thoughts and perceptions that our answers can be regarded as totally dependable. Second, if we were to put all our marks at the left end of each line, we would certainly be suspected of wearing rose-colored glasses. The fact is that we ourselves, other people, life, and the world are simply not perfect. This is not the best of all possible worlds. Furthermore, our ideas of God are usually distorted by our tendency to humanize God. We make God to our human image and likeness. We tend to project our human limitations upon him. On the other hand, a very small shaded area would probably indicate a very small and painful vision which would result in a small and painful life.

Perhaps it would be interesting and profitable to ask some friend-confidant whose balance, outlook, and judgment seem very sound and reliable to join you in taking this test. If this other person whom you regard as very human and very much alive were to score a profile quite different from your own, it might be helpful to discuss the contrasts, comparing his or her vision with your own. Lastly, if one of the five suggested categories is noticeably different from the others on your test, you might open yourself to be questioned by life in this area. There could well be a cluster of distortions in this area which is limiting your happiness and participation in the fullness of life.

Now let us turn to a review of what some very knowledgeable people regard as the most common and prevalent distortions in the visions of human beings.

Sigmund Freud, as everyone knows, believed that the deepest and most damaging distortions were to be found in the areas of sexual perceptions and aggression (destructive, even violent, behavior directed at others, things, or even self). Freud's onetime disciple, Alfred Adler, proposed that human neurosis is caused by the mistaken belief (misconception) that one must prove his or her personal superiority without regard for the common good.

However, the cognitive approach to human growth and the fullness of life, the development of the misconception hypothesis, and the system of Rational Emotive Therapy is today associated mostly with Albert Ellis (*Reason and Emo-*

tion in Psychotherapy, 1962; and with R. Harper, *A Guide to Rational Living,* 1968). Ellis theorizes that a human being is uniquely rational and irrational. All emotional and psychological problems are traceable to irrational or illogical thinking and ideas. This irrational thinking and the consequent distortion of ideas come mostly from learning experiences in early life, though such experiences are not limited exclusively to childhood. Echoing the ancient Roman philosopher Epictetus (A.D. 50), Ellis maintains that people are not emotionally and psychologically disturbed by events or things but by the views they take of those events or things. For example, being small or sick or bald are not problems in themselves which necessarily result in emotional or psychological disturbance. However, if I distort the significance of these conditions or exaggerate their importance, then I will have painful problems. Consequently, Ellis sees all hope for happiness and a full life in the reorganization of one's thinking.

Though it has not been his main interest to evolve a theory of personality development, Ellis does say that the learning experiences of early childhood have the most profound effect on a person's rational/irrational thinking and behavior. The perpetuation of distorted ideas acquired in childhood is the main source of unhappiness in later life. Since our thoughts or ideas cause our emotions, emotional balance is possible only through the adjustment of one's thinking. It is the faulty interpretation of a situation that leads to emotional and psychological disturbance. Only by disputing the irrational, unrealistic thinking can one be brought to emotional harmony and adjusted behavior.

Ellis rather decisively lists eleven irrational ideas that are most commonly found in emotionally and psychologically disturbed people. The first seven are said to figure most prominently in the development of anxiety. The final four tend rather to produce hostility. I have taken some liberty with the exact choice and order of words used by Ellis. However, the words are almost verbatim, and each idea is substantially that of Ellis. After each of these most common misconceptions I have given a short indication of the distortion found in the idea and a similar indication of a more rational view of the same matter.

1. *I must be loved and approved by everyone in my community, especially by those who are most important to me.*   Any unattainable goal, which leaves one with only the possibility of failure, is an irrational goal. No one will ever be loved and approved universally. The more effort one makes to attain such a goal, the more anxious, frustrated, and self-destructive one will become. A rational orientation in this matter would certainly include the very human desire to be approved and loved. However, I can't get and don't need to have the love and approval of everyone to have a happy and full life. When I am disapproved of, I will examine the validity of the criticism implied in the disapproval to see if the problem is mine or my critic's. If it is mine, I will try to change. If it is my critic's, it is up to him or her to change.

2. *I must be perfectly competent, adequate, and successful in achieving before I can think of myself as worthwhile.*   Another impossible goal is contained in this distortion. It can lead only to constant overexertion in feverish activity, a constant fear of failure, and an inferiority complex. Such compulsive need and striving usually result in psychosomatic sickness and a feeling that I have lost rational control of my life. I have a ring in my nose.

More rationally oriented people want to do well for their own sakes and satisfaction, not in order to be better than others. Rational people also want to enjoy what they undertake, to be led by interest rather than driven by an obsession for success.

3. *I have no control over my own happiness. My happiness is completely in the control of external circumstances.* This distortion is, of course, a lie which I am tempted to tell myself in order to avoid challenge and responsibility. It is sometimes easier to be a martyr—to roll over and play dead—than to reexamine my situation and do whatever I can. The rational person knows that happiness is not determined by outside forces and events. It is rather a matter of attitudes, and these cannot be coerced by outside forces, which at most can be physically afflicting. Happiness or unhappiness is ultimately derived from the way events are perceived, evaluated, and internally verbalized. Happiness does, in fact, come from within, as the sages have been saying for centuries.

4. *My past experiences and the events of my life have determined my present life and behavior. The influence of the past cannot be eradicated.* It is true that we are creatures of habit and that relearning is difficult. The distortion is to believe that it is impossible. This kind of passive acceptance or determinism is often used to avoid the challenge of change. Rational people know the importance of the past and its influences, but they know that they can change by reevaluating those influences, reinterpreting events, and reassessing the perceptions of their original vision. Rational people always remain bigger than their problems.

5. There is one right and perfect solution to each of my problems. If this is not found, it will be devastating for me. It is obviously not true that there is one perfect solution for each problem in life. Furthermore, failure to solve a problem with a perfect solution is not catastrophic. We can learn from and grow because of failure. The anxious attitude implied in this misconception will probably produce such anxiety that problem-solving efficiency will be considerably reduced. A rational person knows that there are options and alternatives in the solution to all problems. It is also true that some problems are insoluble. We must live with them and learn the art of acceptance. When a problem-solving decision is upon them, rational people will consider all the options of the moment and choose the solution that seems most feasible.

6. Dangerous or fearsome things are causes for great concern. I must be prepared for the worst by constantly dwelling on and agonizing over these possible calamities. The deception involved in this irrational thinking is that worry and anxious anticipation somehow help. In fact, they tend to prevent objective evaluation of the possible danger and will diminish the possibility of effective reaction should the calamity occur. Such anxiety and anticipation may even induce the feared situation. Fear tends to make that which we fear come true. Such worry also tends to exaggerate unpleasant events out of all proportion. Every day becomes doomsday. Rational people know that worry does not help, so they invest their energies in an evaluation of the situation and a decision about what can be done to prevent possible tragedy. Rational people do not presume that tragedy will occur. In the case of crippling fears, they will prudently and gradually dispel them by acting against them.

7. *I should be dependent on others and must have someone stronger than myself on whom I can rely.* This distortion is a gross exaggeration of dependency. It leads a life of "being cared for" in place of independence, self-determination, and self-expression. This kind of dependency has a tendency to escalate; I become more and more dependent. And the more dependent I become, the more I am at the mercy of the person on whom I am leaning. Rational individuals want to be their own persons, to make their own decisions, to take their own responsibility. Of course, rational people are willing to ask for and accept help when they need it, but they will turn over their lives to no one. They are willing to take risks. If they are wrong or fail, it is not the end of the world.

8. *If my life does not work out the way I had planned, it will be really terrible. When things go badly for me, it is a catastrophe.* This is a clearly irrational attitude because things very rarely go exactly as planned. This attitude invites frustration as a normal state. Getting upset does not help, but will make the situation worse. Furthermore, this attitude makes the perfect achievement of one's plans a condition for satisfaction and happiness. This is a good formula for frustration and ulcers. Rational people will try to work at the successful implementation of their plans, but will improvise when things do not turn out. They will develop a tolerance for frustration and learn to enjoy the possibilities for growing, learning, and adjusting in situations of reversal. They stay on top of the situation instead of letting the situation bury them.

9. *It is easier to avoid certain difficulties and responsibilities than to face them.* The irrationality of

this idea is that it neglects the fact that avoiding a task or responsibility is often more painful and fatiguing than doing what is required without procrastination. Avoidance always leads to further problems and eventually to loss of self-confidence and self-respect. Rational people spend their energy doing what they can rather than devising escapes. If they fail, they study the causes of the failure and try not to fall into the same traps. Such people know that there is much more pleasure and satisfaction in taking on difficulties and responsibilities than in avoiding them.

10. *Some people are bad, wicked, villainous. They should be blamed and punished.* This distorted idea presumes that we have the ability to judge the responsibility, the conscience, and the knowledge of another. What may appear as evil can be the result of insanity or ignorance. Rational people know they cannot judge persons but only issues. They have no X-ray eyes to see the intention, conscience, or knowledge of another. They confine themselves to an assessment of what is done rather than attempt a judgment of the doer of the deed.

11. *One should be very upset over the problems and disturbances of other people.* The irrationality of this attitude resides in its self-destructiveness and over-eagerness to make the problems of others one's own. This is not to deny a healthy empathy for those who are suffering. However, the only way I am going to be of any help to others is by retaining my own balance and peace of mind. Rational people make a judgment of the situation of their neighbors and try to do whatever they can to help those in need. If nothing can be done, they do not surrender their personal peace to an impossible situation.

Ellis catalogs these eleven major misconceptions into three categories. They are a rough equivalent of the five categories described previously in this book: self, others, life, world, God. Ellis calls these three categories of distortion the "three whines," in each of which something is "awfulized." They are the irrational attitudes that give people trouble.

1. Poor Me! (Awfulizes one's own self.) "Because it would be highly preferable if I were outstandingly competent, I absolutely should and must be; it is awful when I am not, and I am therefore a worthless individual."

2. Poor Stupid Other People! (Awfulizes what others are doing to me.) "Because it is highly desirable that others treat me considerately and fairly, they absolutely should and must, and they are rotten people who deserve to be utterly damned when they do not."

3. Poor Stupid Life and Universe! (Awfulizes what the world is doing to me and my life situation.) "Because it is preferable that I experience pleasure rather than pain, the world absolutely should arrange this, and life is horrible and I can't bear it when the world doesn't."

Albert Ellis,
"The No Cop-out Therapy,"
Psychology Today, 1973

I have combed through the writings of many authors on this subject of distortions in human thinking. The misconceptions they list are almost always contained in one of the eleven listed by Ellis. Anthropologist Margaret Mead, for example, believes that it is a uniquely American distortion to set impossibly high moral standards that can result only in failure and guilt feelings. Psychiatrist Karen Horney thinks that the "idealized self-image" (the illusory self) as opposed to and in conflict with a realistic self-evaluation is at the bottom of much human misery. Psychologist Victor Raimy adds "the special persons complex," usually found in the favorite child of a coddling mother or someone who has received much public attention and praise, and "phrenophobia," the misconception that one is on the verge of insanity. However, I feel that these and other more specific distortions can be found in the general categories of Ellis.

I would like to conclude this chapter with a list of specific distortions or misconceptions that I have found to be at the root of most neurotic suffering in myself and in others. The list is by no means exhaustive. We are all, as Ellis says, uniquely rational and irrational. My distortions are as uniquely mine as my fingerprints. Still, we are all somewhat alike. There is a human unity in our diversity. Consequently, some of these listed misconceptions may look or sound a bit familiar. A study and discussion of these misconceptions might prove personally profitable. It will be a time to practice flexibility and the openness of being questioned by life. I trust that the meaning of and distortion in each of the following will be reasonably clear.

1. I have received so much that I have no right to have any faults.

2. I have only myself to blame.

3. I cannot be angry at anyone but myself.

4. My physical dimensions are the measure of my virility or femininity.

5. Nobody could really love me.

6. I don't deserve to be happy.

7. Loving yourself or admitting your talents is egotistical and conceited.

8. What really matters is *ME!* I am a special person.

9. Self-forgiveness is self-indulgence.

10. I am a born loser.

11. Laughing at yourself is stupid and self-demeaning.

12. I have to bury forever many of my memories; they would make me too angry or sad.

13. If I begin reflecting on my past, it will be like opening a Pandora's box; it is better to leave well enough alone.

14. If I ever begin to release my emotions, I know I will lose control.

15. Keep your mouth shut, and you won't get into trouble.

16. People make me mad or afraid.

17. Stupidity makes me angry.

18. Hurting the feelings of others should always be avoided.

19. My thoughts and feelings would really shock you.

20. Keeping the peace is the most important thing in a relationship.

21. You can't say what you really think and feel.

22. You can't really trust anyone.

23. My parents were ideal in every way.

24. I know that if people get to know the real me, they will not like me.

25. I must play a role in order to be accepted by others.

26. I have to be the center of attention or I don't enjoy myself.

27. Because I play roles in front of people to impress them, I am phoney and therefore no good at all.

28. My parents are to blame for me.

29. Marriage is only a piece of paper.

30. Love does not last.

31. Do your thing, Baby! You're the only one that counts.

32. You can always tell a hypocrite.

33. You have to give in—to compromise yourself—in order to get along with people.

34. If someone comes to me with a problem, I must do more than just listen and discuss the problem.

35. Love is all sweetness and light; when a person has found love, it is the end of all struggle and suffering.

36. What will the neighbors say? We have to look good.

37. Perfect love is the only kind of real love.

38. I do not need others.

39. I know what is best for you.

40. Love is doing whatever the beloved wants.

41. If you want something done, you have to do it yourself.

42. I know your whole trouble.

43. I'll get even if it's the last thing I do.

44. You can't praise others too much; it will go to their heads.

45. Love is blind.

46. I have to please others in order to satisfy their expectations of me.

47. No commitment can be for life.

48. This is the way I am and always will be.

49. I just can't decide.

50. It's no use trying.

51. I just don't have the will power; I can't.

52. It's easier just to give in.

53. Where there's a will there's a way. You can do anything you really want to do.

54. I have to prove myself.

55. Life is one "damn thing" after another.

56. I must win them all. I must be Hertz, not Avis.

57. A true ideal should always be just out of reach.

58. Life is easier if you don't stop to think about it.

59. Good people do not suffer. Virtue always triumphs in the end.

60. Those were the good old days.

61. You only go around once. Grab all you can for yourself.

62. We are for time, not time for us. We must keep moving and producing to justify our existence.

63. You cannot set your sights too high.

64. Whatever you do, you should do it perfectly.

65. Never give up.

66. A thing is either black or white. To make distinctions is always confusing.

67. Beauty is in the eye of the beholder.

68. The world owes me a living.

69. I can't waste time taking a walk, reading a book, or puttering in a garden.

70. Every problem is solvable.

71. The world belongs to the young. Ah, to be young again!

72. Failure is failure and all failure is final.

73. I'm too old to start now.

74. Who needs God?

75. Prayer is for the weak.

A new life through a new vision

Man alone,
of all the creatures of the earth,
can change his own pattern.
Man alone is the architect
of his destiny.
The greatest discovery in our generation
is that human beings,
by changing the inner attitudes
of their minds,
can change the outer aspects
of their lives.

William James,
The Principles of Psychology

Of all the aspects of the misconception hypothesis and the system of Rational Emotive Therapy, certainly the most appealing is its fundamental assumption that *we can change.* Our lives are, to a very great extent, in our own hands. My personal instincts and intuition rebel against the deterministic, fatalistic psychologies which make us passive puppets and make our lives phonograph records playing out a preestablished program. In accepting the misconception hypothesis we accept, to a great extent, personal responsibility for our destiny. We are not prisoners of the past. We are pioneers of an exciting future.

Let us now very briefly review the main principles of the misconception hypothesis and vision therapy.

1. Misconceptions (also called "distortions" or "delusions") are mistaken beliefs, faulty ideas, unrealistic and unhealthy attitudes. They usually come in clusters since one misconception frequently leads to other related misconceptions in the same area. There are five general categories to be considered: self, other people, life, the world, and God.

2. Some misconceptions are relatively harmless, or benign, because they do not noticeably affect emotional or behavior patterns. Other distortions are crippling, or malignant, because they produce painful and negative emotional patterns which are disruptive of the whole personality and of social adjustment.

3. Misconceptions must be identified before one can work at their elimination. When identified properly and adequately, misconceptions are always specific and concrete. For example: "I have to be

approved by everybody or I question my own
worth." Vague and unspecified delusions are usually worthless abstractions designed to obscure the
real problem. For example: "I think I have a tendency to think too much."

4. A person can find a happy and fully human life only
   to the extent that these crippling misconceptions
   are recognized and then modified or eliminated.

5. When a person recognizes one of his or her delusions or misconceptions, it is a moment of insight.
   What actually happens in such insights is that we
   see, sometimes very suddenly, the distortion in the
   way we were interpreting the evidence of personal
   experience. We see that we were incorrectly put-
   ting together the pieces of the reality picture.

6. The more flexible and open people are, the more
   insights they will acquire. Their emotional patterns
   and ability to participate in a fully human life will
   improve and grow with each new insight.

7. Insights can come at any time and under any circumstances. There is no one sure way to acquire
   new insights, although there are recommended
   procedures that facilitate insight for most people.

8. The system for eliminating misconceptions
   through insight which we have devised and are
   proposing is called "vision therapy." It is a self-help
   method of growth. It will be described in complete
   detail in this chapter.

9. The misconception hypothesis and the system of
   vision therapy do not regard emotions as the

ultimate area of consideration or concentration. Emotions are only indicators. Habitual patterns of negative emotions are always a signal of some underlying misconception. The target of achievement is the elimination of such misconceptions through insight and the acquisition of healthy, realistic attitudes in the place of these misconceptions. It may be that some discharge of pent-up emotions will be necessary before some people are able to come to needed insights.

10. Success at vision therapy is measured by satisfaction and by growth into a fully human and joyful life. Such progress in turn can be more specifically measured by growth in positive, life-giving attitudes toward self, others, life, the world, and God. The composite of all these attitudes is a person's vision, the way he or she sees reality. It is this vision that determines the emotional patterns of one's life. Only if this vision is sound and healthy can a person enjoy a truly happy and fully human life.

Having summarized the main principles of the misconception hypothesis and vision therapy, we return now to the particular system of Albert Ellis, which is based on the misconception hypothesis. When Ellis summarizes his own system of Rational Emotive Therapy, he calls it the ABC system. In every human reaction there is an Activating event, a Belief system through which the event is interpreted and evaluated, and a Consequent set of emotional reactions. Ellis is critical of many other systems of psychotherapy because they seem to concentrate on the A and C, while neglecting the B, which is the central concern of Rational Emotive Therapy. Very simply, the same thing presumably happens to many persons but the results or emotional reactions are often very different. Some people have enormous coping ability and powers of resilience. Others go into a tailspin over trifles. Obviously, something comes into play after the activating event which accounts for the great differences of reaction. This is what Ellis calls a "belief system" and which we have been calling a "vision." Let us look at a diagram:

A: Activating event
Someone unfairly and harshly criticizes me and professes dislike for me.

B: Belief system
I must be loved and approved by everybody or I lose all sense of my own worth.

C: Consequent emotions
Poor me! Depression, sadness.

Ellis has recently filled out his schematic with two more letters, adding that if we are to restore rationality to our belief system and emotional peace to our souls, we must:

D: Dispute the distorted, irrational misconception in the belief system.
I don't have to please everyone, to be loved and approved, in order to retain a sense of personal worth. My critic has the problem, not I.

E: Event or experience is transformed by reinterpretation and reevaluation, which makes possible the elimination of the misconception.
Different emotional reaction: continued self-confidence, personal peace, and compassion for the critic.

I would strongly agree with Ellis that not only many systems of psychotherapy but also most people in their daily lives are concerned only with the A (Activated event) and C (Consequent emotions). In the wake of strong and negative emotions most of us do not attempt any kind of a vision-therapy investigation of our belief systems. We make little or no effort to find out what is in us that has caused such emotions to arise. We know that there are probably many other people who would not react as we do to a given stimulus, but we still do not accept the challenge to check our vision. We are tempted to pass it off with a bromide such as: "This is the way I am." Or, "Sorry, but this is me!" Some of us even try to recreate others in our own image and likeness by thinking that everyone really reacts as we do, but some just don't show it.

Remember that every activating event has to flow through the filter system of your own uniquely rational/irrational belief system. The consequent emotions are not determined by the activating event but by the belief system. However, there is always hope, even if the emotional patterns are habitually and painfully negative. It is within our power to dispute our belief systems, locating and eliminating specific misconceptions and consequently transforming the events and experiences of our lives.

Let us look at another diagram:

A: Activating event of failure (at school, in work, in carrying out plans, etc.).

B: Belief that failure indicates something is missing in me. My personal value is undermined and permanently damaged by failure.

C: Consequent sadness, depression, discouragement.

D. Dispute of misconception: I reevaluate and em-
phatically deny that failure is an exposé of personal
worthlessness. Failure does not diminish my person.
The only real mistake is the one from which we
learn nothing. It is true that my efforts resulted
in failure, but I myself am not a failure. Everyone
fails. The successful person is one who profits
from failure.

E. Event of failure has been reevaluated and transformed into a profitable experience and time of
growth. Because of the changed interpretation of
the event, the emotional reaction is likewise
changed from a "this is the end" depression to a
"wait till next time" eagerness and enthusiasm.

Unfortunately, diagraming is easier than doing. Since
the main problem in any "doing" is a positive intention and
determination, we must now take up the question of motivation. We have already described the counterproductive
reluctance that almost everybody feels to challenge his or
her own presuppositions. The old vision, for better or for
worse, has served long and well. It has given life predictability and given us consistency instead of chaos. The old
is always safe even if sad. The new is untested. How are
people led to a desire for change and growth? How can
they be convinced that the benefits of a new and fuller life
through a new and fuller vision are really worth the price
demanded?

People who go to professionals for help usually go because their negative emotional patterns have become too
painful or because their world seems to be falling apart.
The first problem encountered in helping such people is
the period of disintegration or disorientation experienced

in the stepping from the old into the new. It is a limbo of uncertainty and chaos. Still, pain is very persuasive. Individuals who have had enough struggling, depression, constant anxiety, or smoldering hostility may have hit bottom and be ready to rebound. They may be ready to make the effort, to take the risks of thinking and acting in new ways. However, some people have "low bottoms" and have to fall apart pretty badly before they are willing to put the pieces together in a new and different pattern. Other people have "high bottoms" and are ready for change. They sense that the course they are on will lead only to a sad nowhere. They are ready for reevaluation, for a new vision.

Then there are the children of the new beatitude: Blessed are those who hunger after life in all its fullness! They have no appetite or willingness to settle for mediocrity in any form. These are the pioneer people who write new songs, study new theories, and build better mousetraps. They can be found in offices, schools, factories, or supermarkets, but there is always something of a mountain climber in their blood. They say an expansive "Yes!" to life and "Amen!" to love. They are ready to reexamine their belief systems. They are ready for vision therapy and anything else that promises growth. For them, to stop growing is to stop living. When you're through growing, you're through!

So I suppose that the sales pitch for vision therapy would go something like this: Have you had it with depression, anxiety, loneliness, and hostility? Are you tired of lifelong difficulties and endless struggle? Wouldn't you really rather uncover the roots of your painful emotions than live with them in an endurance contest? If you are the enthusiastic type, do you want to make your life an exciting adventure, to walk into a world of wider dimensions and brighter colors? Are you ready to join the dance and sing the songs of a more human and fuller life? Are you open to the idea that the difference between what you are and what you can be is a matter of ideas, insights, a belief system, a vision? If you are either of these two people, please keep reading.

The journey into a fully human, fully alive existence requires certain supplies and equipment. They are all, in varying degrees, necessary. Please read the list carefully and set yourself to acquire whatever you do not have.

1. *Openness and Flexibility.* You must believe with all your heart that you do not possess all truth in proper perspective. You must be ready to be questioned by life. Of course, every day, every event, and every person that touches your consciousness is questioning you. Do you love yourself? Can you enjoy yourself? What do you think of failure? Have you really recognized humanity and individuality in other people? Have you made the discovery of otherness? Do you like most people, or are they a bother? The first requirement to achieve a new life through a new vision is a readiness to hear and to attempt to answer the questions that life will ask you.

2. *Sensory and Emotional Awareness.* It is necessary that you learn how to listen to your senses, and to register consciously the sights, sounds, smells, tastes, and touches of daily life. You will have to hear what your body is saying: when it is tired and when it is tense. This physical awareness is a prerequisite for emotional awareness because every emotion is a perceptual-physiological reality. In other words, an emotion exists partly in the mind and partly in the body. Fritz Perls, the late and great Gestalt therapist, insisted that "awareness of the new," of sensory input, is "sufficient to solve all neurotic difficulties" (*Gestalt Therapy Now: Theory, Techniques, Application,* edited by Fagan and Shepherd).

It is this sensory awareness that will lead us to our deepest feelings unless we employ some kind of blockage or denial. Jittery nerves, fatigue, and other bodily conditions can become for us direct avenues to emotional awareness. As was said, every emotion by its very nature is partly physiological. The physical reactions are usually like the top of the iceberg, the part that shows.

In whatever way we can, with whatever techniques prove helpful, we must learn to be in touch with our feelings or emotions. This is a complicated achievement, which I have treated at length in two other books and can only touch upon here. (Please see *Why Am I Afraid to Tell You Who I Am?* and *The Secret of Staying in Love,* both published by Tabor Publishing.)

All recent psychological theories of emotion assume that our emotional reactions depend on our interpretation and appraisal of the situation in which the emotions arise. The way we perceive the situation is in fact an intrinsic part of the emotion itself because emotions are mental-physical realities. Consequently, when people explore their deepest feelings, they are simultaneously exploring their deepest thoughts and convictions because emotions are partly perceptual. Even though it may seem difficult to believe, there is no time in a conscious state when we are without any emotions because there is no time when we are not thinking. Much of the time our emotional reactions are so slight that we are not even aware of them. However, a sensitive polygraph (lie-detector) machine would register these constant emotional reactions. Such a machine even picks up physiological reactions to recited words like "mother . . . father . . . love . . . war . . . sex." The point is that if we are to become aware of our belief systems or visions, it is essential that we be attuned to our emotional reactions.

As we have said previously, all negative emotions, but especially anxiety and hostility, are signals of a malignant misconception somewhere in our total vision. We cannot afford to pass over such reactions with a comment that we will probably feel better tomorrow or with a belief that we would be all right if only we could get a good night's sleep. All negative feelings, from the mildest discomfort to the deepest depression, will lead us to a moment of insight if only we will follow.

This is even true in what is called "free-floating anxiety," which is supposedly a state of fearful apprehension without attachment to a definite object of fear. Many psychologists, however, maintain that when a person begins to describe his or her individual experience of this anxiety, a very definite fear and misconception will emerge.

3. *A Friend-Confidant.* A person with whom we can be totally open is for many reasons an absolute requirement for growth into the fullness of life. However, there are special reasons why such a friend-confidant is essential for the successful practice of vision therapy. First of all, you will remember the statement that for many of us some release of pent-up emotional turbulence is necessary before we can quietly review our belief systems and find the troublesome misconception. Only the kind of friend-confidant suggested here will be willing and able to handle the communication of these emotions. A person less close will probably tell us not to cry or become excited. That person would not know us well enough to know what to anticipate. Such a person would be afraid to give us full freedom to have and express our feelings. Only a true friend-confidant will know and love us enough to provide this liberty of experience and expression.

Alfred Adler says that a warm human relationship is necessary to give people the courage needed to face and understand their mistakes. Knowing that someone loves us unconditionally enables us to face and admit our delusions. This is also one of the main principles of Carl Rogers in his theory of counseling. We can understand and accept ourselves realistically only when someone outside ourselves first understands and accepts us. Consequently, Adler and others recommend that if a person does not have and cannot make such a friend, he or she might have to join some kind of a warm and receptive group.

Dialogue and discussion with such a friend-confidant make still another very definite contribution in helping us to locate our misconceptions. We have to organize a problem before we can talk it over with another. Very often, if left to ourselves, we do not go through this organization of the problem and its ramifications. Our problems remain vague and diffuse when kept inside us. With a friend-confidant we must not only organize but also verbalize the problem. This reality of verbalization is extremely important. The way we verbalize a situation often determines how we will evaluate it. Very often our reactions are determined by the words we choose to describe the situation. We think in words, plan our lives with words, and tend to be very much defined by our own verbalizations. This is why some have recommended repeating at regular daily intervals positive words or mottoes such as "I am! I can! I will!" If we are interpreting and verbalizing a given situation in a lop-sided manner, dialogue with a friend will tend to help us back to balance and objectivity.

4. *A Journal.* In her book *Widow,* Lynn Caine has a chapter called "Dear Paper Psychiatrist." The reference is to a journal which she kept after the death of her husband. Recording the events of her life and emotional reactions seems to have helped her in the several ways that it can help all of us. A journal provides an outlet for emotional expression, but it also requires the kind of organization and verbalization described above. For most of us the appearance of a blank piece of paper is less threatening than a human face staring at us, waiting for words. We are less inhibited with a paper psychiatrist than with a real one.

Once we have put down the main activating event of a given day, together with our spontaneous emotional reactions, we can go back either at that time or at a later time of quiet and do a little vision therapy. We can check out and challenge the validity of the belief system or vision between the event and our emotional reaction to it. If people were regularly to practice this kind of gentle but persistent self-examination of their vision, I am sure they would find, as I have, many new insights and an immediate change in the emotional patterns of their lives. Obviously, the more precise and vivid the verbalization in writing of this kind, the greater the likelihood that misconceptions will surface for recognition.

The following is an excerpt from my own attempts at keeping a journal. It may have some illustrative value.

Tonight, as I was finishing my speech, I was suddenly interrupted by a shouted question. I could hear the

edges of anger on the words of the person speaking.
After asking his question the questioner started to
leave angrily, but then decided to stay. It was the first
time this has ever happened to me. I was flustered,
angry and suddenly felt very competitive. It was no
longer a sharing situation. This was win/lose. I hate
to lose at anything. Adrenalin. The flushed feeling. I
never did get to finish my talk. The ending was impressive, too, and might have made a difference. Who
knows now? Other questions followed. Some of
them were vague but unfriendly questions. I'm not
used to this. I almost always get hugs and standing
ovations. Failure really stops me cold. And I think
that speaking is my greatest talent, too. Afterward,
when the adrenalin stopped, I felt like the little boy
who stubbed his toe: It hurt too much to laugh but
I was too old to cry. Sad. Hurt. Mad. Questioning
myself, my intelligence, confidence in my presenta-
tion. I needed to and did talk it over with a friend. I
couldn't take all those heavy emotions to bed with
me. Tomorrow, of course, all the pain will be drained
out, though I will remember, maybe angrily. I'm
really glad I've got that twenty-four hour shut-off
built into my negative emotions. After twenty-four
hours, nothing is worth that much anguish. But what
is in me? Why do I so hate failure? Was tonight really
a failure? Is it that I was speaking about a cause in
which I believe with all my heart or was it my pride
that I was protecting? Or both?

I think I play at being much more confident in
myself than I really am. My illusory self. He's got it
made. The "real me" doesn't. That guy who interrupted me was really rude. He must have problems.

Why don't I feel sorry for him instead of angry at him? Apparently, I think I've got to win them all. Success and self-esteem must be welded together in my mind. Failure really rocks my sense of worth. Tomorrow the dust will be settled, and maybe I'll be able to see more clearly. I know that there is some delusion roaming around inside me. I want to find it. Maybe I have already found it. Maybe the answer is in what I have written here. When I reread this later, perhaps I'll know for sure. If I learn something, I will probably be glad that the whole thing happened. Maybe.

Morning after reflections: My sense of self-worth is threatened by any hostile criticism. I still do not distinguish very well, in cases of criticism, whether the problem is mine or that of the other person. I hold people responsible and accountable for what they do and say. I leave small margins for ignorance and irresistible impulses. I take criticisms personally. My person, not my opinions, is attacked. There is a strange identity in my mind between my person and my opinions.

I would strongly recommend the use of such a journal every day but especially on those days when emotions have been vibrating uncomfortably. The journal should be kept strictly private if the thought of sharing it with a friend-confidant would in a way diminish openness and honesty. The much better thing, of course, would be sharing the contents of the journal with a friend. Two heads are always better than one in matters like this. Dialogue has a way of illuminating the darkened corners of consciousness and awareness.

5. *Times of Quiet Reflection.* Those who write on the subject of misconceptions are fairly unanimous in agreeing that it is the presence of "threat" in some form that tends to cause and to camouflage distortions in vision. Confrontation with threat usually constricts vision. When we are threatened, we instinctively throw up defenses, and this almost always means that we will exclude certain evidence being presented to us (selective inattention). This new evidence might force us to reevaluate our vision, and to admit delusion. It might challenge us to begin thinking and acting in a new way. We tend to become more defensive than perceptive.

It would be ideal if a person could reserve some time at the end of each day to relax, review, and reevaluate. Most of us, however, are too much in the clutches of clock and calendar. But there are times such as train rides, while waiting for sleep, walking to and from stores, when we are waiting for someone who has been delayed, and so forth. At these times threat is usually minimal and vision can be expanded to receive new insights. Such times are invaluable for growth into a fuller and more peaceful life.

6. *The Stretch Marks of Risk and Revision.* There is no question that we must act on insights if they are to become the new habits of thinking that will replace our old delusions. Insights demand more than lip service. They demand allegiance. Insights need the support of emotional strength. They must be incorporated into one's life-style. No new truth is ever really learned until it is acted upon. This means some inner crinkling and crunch: stretch marks.

For example, let us suppose that I think of myself as "a problem-solver to the world." It is my vocation. Then I come to the insight that being a problem-solver is irrational. First, it presumes that other people are not big enough, old enough, or smart enough to solve their own problems. Second, to solve another's problem only aids and abets his or her indecisiveness and immaturity. It cultivates in that person an exaggerated sense of dependency on the advice-giver. Lastly, being a problem-solver is an unrealistic and exhausting burden for anyone to carry. It is foolish to play Atlas holding up the whole world.

The true test of change and growth will come the next time some dependent and indecisive person pathetically whimpers: "What should I do? Please tell me." It will take real determination to act on my insight, to step out of the old rut and say: "I don't know what you should do. What do you think you should do?"

There is another aspect of learning and doing. Actual doing obviously completes the learning process. However, it also works in reverse. Doing very often initiates a learning process. Suppose, for example, I am firmly convinced that I cannot give a speech in public or take unsatisfactory goods back to the salesperson. So what should I do? So I should swallow hard and do it! Yes, just do it. I must act against my phobias. Only in doing it will I learn that I *can* do it and thereby dispatch another delusion. Every day we should all do something that will extend us; we should win little victories over our fears that will widen the world and our lives. We will gradually learn in this way about the undreamed-of potentialities which we had all the time but never used.

Is there a person you cannot bring yourself to contradict? Have you really never cried in front of other people? Can you complain (politely, of course) to the landlord? Are there certain decisions you can never make without getting confirmation from another? Is there really some secret and haunting fear which you have never confided to anyone? When the opportune moment occurs, just do it. Win a victory over yourself, widen your vision and your world, walk into a new and fuller life.

I'm sure you know that all the principles and calculations of aerodynamics, as my friend Mark Link has pointed out, deny the bumblebee any right to fly. With his flimsy wings and short wingspread, the experts say, he just shouldn't get his husky body off the ground. It is certainly a good thing that bumblebees don't know this. Believing in limitations without testing them can become a self-fulfilling prophecy. As long as you think you can't, you can't. So don't let anyone else tell you, and above all don't tell yourself, that you can't. Learn that you can by doing it. (Note: I do not mean *flying*.) Practice disbelieving all the old lies and distortions that you have been telling yourself and leaving unchallenged.

7. *Daily Exercise.* Emotions are most easily recognized and explored while we are experiencing them. Memory is selective. It almost always dulls and distorts. Because emotions are a perceptual-physical reality, our perceptions and our vision are built right into our emotions. Consequently, one's belief system is uniquely available for inspection at the very moment of emotional turbulence. Insights are perhaps more available to us after some emotional clearance and in a setting that is threat-free and conducive to reflection. However, there is a distinct opportunity for insight during the emotional vibration precisely because our emotions are most real and undistorted for us at that moment. It is a valuable time for on-the-spot vision therapy.

I know from personal experience that when practiced with a friend-confidant and in a journal, one can develop considerable facility for this on-the-spot vision therapy. It soon becomes a way of life and its benefits are soon evident. Sensory and emotional awareness, as described, come first. There must be a constantly renewed intention to practice and cultivate such awareness. Then we must go on to a gentle but persistent inspection of the vision or belief system. Remember that there is no time when we are not experiencing some kind of emotional reaction. Consider these reactions:

I feel shy, withdrawn.	Why?
I feel like a failure, guilty.	Why?
I feel attacked.	Why?
I feel strangely sad.	Why?
I really enjoy this attention.	Why?
That remark really hurt me.	Why?

Conclusion: For the average person to continue any practice over a long period of time, he or she must derive a satisfaction or experience a success greater than the price of effort paid. Certainly for extended use of vision therapy, if not for even the most modest beginning, there will have to be some satisfaction or success. I personally very much hunger for the full human life, and of course I want to find the wrinkles of irrationality that diminish my participation in such a life. As I continue to practice what I am here preaching, I am aware of increasing peace and joy in my life. But more immediately and practically I find daily vision therapy very interesting. I have found out that I am interesting, complicated, uniquely rational, and uniquely irrational. I have come to a much deeper understanding of my past and present. I eagerly await the future. And most of all, I have come to like myself much better by being this kind of interested, curious, and helpful friend to myself. I am sure that you will have the same experience.

*   *   *

Suggested Exercises in Vision Therapy

1. Record in writing (a journal?) the strongest negative emotion that you have experienced recently. Describe the activating event and your consequent emotions.

   a. Study your verbalization of the event. For example: Your car has broken down. You can either say: "Well, this is certainly an inconvenience, but I am sure it will all work out." Or you can say: "Oh my God! This is all I need. What a way to ruin a day." Study the relationship between the words you chose to describe the event and your emotional reactions.

   b. Ask yourself what there is in your vision of reality that resulted in your precise emotional reaction. Is there a distortion or misconception in your vision that threw the whole event out of focus?

2. Try this experiment with your friend-confidant. Both of you write what you would guess are your own five basic misconceptions. For example: "I have to be approved and loved by everyone in order to retain a sense of personal worth." Then both of you write what you would guess are the five basic misconceptions of the other person. Finally, share and discuss what has been written. Note:

Do not proceed with this experiment if there is any feeling such as: "I've been waiting a long time to lay this on you!" Review and revise the distortion under that hostility before attempting this exercise. Such guessing and sharing have to be acts of love or they will be counterproductive. Adler and others have found that this exercise of guessing opens a person to the recognition of misconceptions. This has worked very well for me.

3. Take an area of recurrent negative emotions, especially of anger and fear. For example: "I get furious while driving if someone cuts in ahead of me." Or, "When people disagree with me on an important issue, I get very upset and I stay very upset for a long time."

   Ask yourself about your inner vision. What is in you, in your belief system, that makes this situation so disturbing? For example: "I see all other drivers as my competitors. If a man cuts in ahead of me, it is one point for him and none for me." Or, "I think only of myself because I am a 'special person.' I do not consider that he may be on his way to the hospital, to a sick wife or injured child." Or, "When people disagree with me, I always suspect it is because they do not like me. If they liked me, they wouldn't disagree with me."

4. Here are ten principles of full human living. After each principle are questions. Using the techniques of vision therapy, write or describe to a friend-confidant somewhat lengthy answers to the questions. The "Why?" at the end asks you to explain your answers in terms of your basic vision or belief

system. Your answers should come from an examination of that vision.

Principle One: Be yourself. Don't wear a mask or play a role.

> ***Question:*** In what circumstances do you find it most difficult to be honest and open about what you think and feel? Why?

Principle Two: Experience fully and express freely your true emotions.

> ***Question:*** With which emotions are you most uncomfortable? Which emotions do you feel least free to express? Why?

Principle Three: Do not let fear of hurting another's feelings make your decisions or prevent you from doing or saying what you think you should.

> ***Question:*** Are there special persons or types of persons or special situations in which this fear of hurting another's feelings is crippling and painful to you? Why?

Principle Four: Assert yourself. You have a right to be respected, to think your own thoughts and make your own choices. You should be listened to and taken seriously. Insist on this right.

> ***Question:*** When and with whom do you find it hardest to be assertive? To demand respect for your person and rights? Why?

Principle Five: Do not bend yourself out of shape trying to please everyone all the time.

Question: Do you feel compelled to please all people or at least certain special people all the time? In certain circumstances? Why?

Principle Six: Do not attempt to make yourself look better by attacking, cutting down, or gossiping about others.

Question: Do you feel threatened by the success of others? Of those with whom you work? Of the same or opposite sex? Do you feel compelled to point out their limitations? Why?

Principle Seven: Look for what is good in others; enjoy and praise others for their good qualities and deeds.

Question: Do you tend to be more aware of others' irritating and obnoxious qualities or their good and pleasing qualities? Do you tend to fix upon the limitations and failures of any particular individual or group? Why?

Principle Eight: Think of yourself in positive terms. Become aware of everything that is good in you.

Question: Are you uncomfortable in describing your achievements or admitting the things you really like about yourself? Within yourself? When talking to others? Why?

Principle Nine: Be gentle and understanding with yourself, as you would like to be with others.

Question: What weakness in yourself most exasperates you? Why?

Principle Ten: Do not judge another's account-ability and subjective guilt. Forgive wherever necessary. Bearing a grudge is self-destructive.

Question: Is there someone you cannot forgive? Why? Is there something that people do which you cannot forgive? Why?

5. Write a verbal portrait of your illusory self, the public image or person you would like others to see, believe in, and be impressed by, but which is not the real you.

Why does this person appeal to you?

6. Evaluate yourself on these five common personality problems by listing them in the order in which you most painfully experience them.

Oversensitivity	Suspiciousness
Resentfulness	Being overly critical
Irritability	

Then take the first two and try to describe, in terms of your basic vision, why you are more troubled by these two problems.

7. What is your basic question or mind-set in approaching life, the persons and events of life? Describe it precisely. For example: "What do I have to fear?" Explain it in terms of your basic vision. *Note:* Do this either in your journal or with a friend-confidant.

8. Do you tend to live (think, daydream) more in the past, present, or future? Why? (See *Note* of number 7.)

9. Describe the person you would like to be. If you were asked why you haven't become this person, how would you answer? What is in your vision or belief system that keeps you from realizing this ideal? (See *Note* of number 7.)

10. Successful vision therapy is based on repetition. Just as we have repeatedly thought the distorted thoughts until they became habitual distortions in our vision, so we must now think the right thoughts, the rational and realistic thoughts, until they become new attitudes replacing the old distortions.

Go back to your five basic misconceptions (number 2, above) and write out the positive, rational thought that would be an appropriate corrective for each misconception. Try to verbalize these corrective thoughts into a motto or resolution which you can repeat internally on those occasions when the old delusion would have crippled you and destroyed your peace. For example: "I am a good person whether everyone approves of me or not."

Vision therapy and religious faith
An appendix for believers

*If you were to take the sum total
of all the authoritative articles
ever written by the most qualified
of psychologists and psychiatrists
on the subject of mental hygiene—
if you were to combine them
and refine them
and cleave out the excess verbiage—
if you were to . . .
have these unadulterated bits
of pure scientific knowledge
concisely expressed
by the most capable of living poets,
you would have an awkward
and incomplete summation
of the Sermon on the Mount.*

Psychiatrist James T. Fisher,
*A Few Buttons Missing:
The Case Book of a Psychiatrist*

One of the main assumptions of the misconception hypothesis and vision therapy is that there is a knowable "reality." We need some version of reality by which we can judge the rationality of our thoughts and to which we can conform our vision or belief system. But who is to say what reality is? Cynics are sure that they are in touch with reality in suspecting everything, trusting no one. Naive persons are convinced that everybody is really a true-blue Boy or Girl Scout at heart. Poets swoon at the beauty of a lake or forest. Others see only a lot of water or lumber. What is reality? Who has conceived it correctly? Who has misconceived it?

Psychologists are reasonable and honest in facing this problem. There are many slightly different solutions. Some suggest that we use a "universal consensus": Reality is that which most people think it is. There are others who offer the pragmatic solution of "what works" as a criterion of reality. There are still others who speak only of an "individual and personal" reality, suggesting that each person has his or her own reality. It is true, of course, that all of us perceive reality, whatever it is, in our own uniquely rational and uniquely irrational ways.

But the practical question persists. How am I to see other human beings? Are we really brothers and sisters in a human family, or are we enemies on a common battlefield? Is there such a thing as a free commitment of love, or are we really determined and predestined to become whatever it is that we will become? Is life governed by the pleasure principle, the power principle, or the programming principle? Is this life all that there is, or is there really a glorious hereafter? Perhaps the answers to these questions would not make a radical difference in my life-style, but they would definitely have some influence on my thoughts, choices, and perspectives. But in these matters, who is to say?

Those who believe in revealed religions have a very definite criterion of reality. They are convinced that God himself has told us in his revelation some very important things about who he is, who we are, about our relationship to one another, about the purpose of life and the significance of this world. There is no logic, of course, either to prove or disprove the authenticity of this revelation of God. Ultimately, the test of faith is always religious experience, which is highly personal and individual. Most believers have at some time felt the touch of God, a conversion-to-faith experience in which they have found a new and distinct peace, power, and presence. The intuition of faith, in this moment, surpasses the reach of all natural logic and scientific knowledge.

This has certainly been my experience, as I have related it in my book *He Touched Me*. Because of my own religious background and personal experience I have accepted the message of Jesus Christ as the master vision of reality. For me the message and person of Jesus are the source of objectification for my own vision of reality. They are the basic norm for my judgments and choices. I have chosen to live my life in the light of this revelation. I want to be God's man and to do God's work: I want to help build a world of love and a human family of mutual understanding.

An evangelist friend of mine told me that when Jesus became real to him as a teenager, he sneaked into his high-school classroom before the start of the school day and printed on the chalkboard in huge letters: JESUS CHRIST IS THE ANSWER! When he returned later with the other students for the beginning of class, he discovered that someone else had printed under his statement: YEAH, BUT WHAT IS THE QUESTION? "Yeah," he thought, "what is the question?"

As his life progressed, my friend found that there isn't only one question. As psychiatrist Viktor Frankl says it should, life asks many different questions of us. Life asks how much we can love, how much we can enjoy and endure. Life asks us if we love ourselves and if we love our fellow human beings. Daily living asks us to distinguish between what is really important and what is unimportant in life: to choose priorities. Life demands that we exercise the judgment of conscience: to choose whatever seems right and to avoid whatever seems wrong. Perhaps the most profound question asked by life is the question of significance and meaning. All of us have to find some purpose or mission in life which will confer upon us a sense of personal distinction and worth. We need to believe that our lives will make a difference for someone or for something.

Of course, there are no patented, simple answers that flow out of automated machines. The German poet Rainer Maria Rilke counsels us to be patient toward all that is unsolved in our hearts. He suggests that we must learn to love the questions themselves while waiting for and working out the answers. Growth is always a gradual process even if there are glittering moments of insight and a divine revelation.

Aleksandr Solzhenitsyn ended his Nobel lecture on literature with the Russian proverb: "One word of truth outweighs the whole world." Saint John, in the prologue of his Gospel, says that the one Word of truth has been spoken by God:

> In the beginning was the Word.
> The Word was with God.
> The Word was God. . . .
> All that came to be had life in him.
> That life was the light of men,
>   a light that darkness could not overpower. . . .
> The Word was made flesh.
> The Word lived among us.
> And we saw his glory . . . full of grace and truth.

My evangelist friend, now an old man, tells me that he now knows much more about the many questions which life asks. Life has questioned him about his values and priorities, about his visions and dreams, about his courage and capacity to love. "But," he said to me, looking over his glasses, "to all the questions life asks: Jesus Christ *is* the answer!"

I am sure that he is right. Of course, this does not imply that the answers which Jesus applied to the problems of his life and times can be imported and applied without any change to the problems of our very different lives and times. Jesus asks us to be as concerned and loving to our world and times as he was to his. However, because all conduct ultimately is the result of a vision, the important thing is to grasp the basic vision of reality that Jesus had, his inner attitudes and belief system. This is the ultimate source of human health and happiness. These Jesus has communicated to us through his message and in his person:

> I am the light of the world.
> Anyone who follows me
> will not be walking in darkness.
> He will have the light of life.
>   **John 8:12**

There is an interesting dialogue between Jesus and his contemporaries recorded in the eighth chapter of John's Gospel. Jesus makes the point that only the truth, the full acceptance of reality, can make a person free.

> If you make my message [vision] the rule of your life, you will then know the truth and the truth will make you free!

When his hearers profess puzzlement at this idea of liberation by truth, pointing out that they have "never been the slaves of anyone," Jesus repeats that he is himself the source of true freedom:

> So if the Son makes you free
> you will really be free!

True health resides principally in one's vision, in one's deepest attitudes; it is not merely the absence of symptoms. Likewise, true freedom has its roots in one's basic vision of reality; it is not merely the absence of coercion from external forces. I see the person of Jesus liberated by a vision that results in a startling freedom: He is free enough to love and to associate with prodigals and prostitutes, and at the end to express a quaking fear and still die freely as an act of love.

> If you make my message [vision] the rule of your life, you will then know the truth and the truth will make you free!

What is the vision of Jesus which lies under his message and manner of life? Whatever else it is, it is certainly a call to the fullness of life.

> I am come that they may have life
> and have it to the full.
> **John 10:10**

At the risk of seeming presumptuous, I would like now to describe some of the central features of the vision of Jesus, as I see them. I think that the message, the life, and the person of Jesus are saying to us:

1. *God is love.* This means that all God does is love. As the sun only shines, conferring its light and warmth on those who stand ready to receive them, so God only loves, conferring his light and warmth on those who would receive them. This means that God does not have anger in him. He does not punish. When we separate ourselves from God and his love by sin, all the change takes place in us, never in him. He is unchangeably loving. Love is sharing, the sharing of one's self and one's life. God's intention in creating us in this world was to share himself and his life with us. In fathering this life in us, God calls us to be his human family, to become a community of love, each wanting and working for the true happiness of all.

2. *You are loved by God, unconditionally and as you are.* God has assured you through his prophets and through his Son that even if a mother were to forget the child of her womb, he would never forget you. Your name is carved in the palms of his hands, inscribed indelibly in his heart. You do not have to win or earn or be worthy of his love. It is a "given." Of course, you can refuse to accept it. You can separate yourself from God's love for a while or even for an eternity. Whatever your response, all during your life and at every moment of your life he will be there offering his love to you, even at those times when you are distracted or refusing it.

Wherever you are in your development, whatever you are doing, with a strong affirmation of all your goodness and good deeds, with a gentle understanding of your weakness, God is forever loving you. You do not have to change, grow, or be good in order to be loved. Rather, you are loved so that you can change, grow, and be good. Your realization of this unconditional love is extremely important. You must remember people like:

> **Peter the Rock,** who was often a sandpile, a loudmouth, a man who had denied even knowing the one who had loved him most.

> **Zacchaeus,** who was a runt, who offered to collect taxes for Rome from his own people for a "kickback" from the take.

> **Mary Magdalene,** who was a "hooker."

> **James and John,** who were mama's boys and pretty ridiculous at times, such as the time when they wanted to destroy a whole town which had given them a poor reception. The "Sons of Thunder," they were laughingly called.

> **Andrew,** who was pretty naive. He thought five loaves and two fish were enough for five thousand people.

> **Thomas,** who was an all-star bullhead.

> **Martha,** who was a twitch, worrier, and complainer.

> **The woman taken in adultery,** who was pretty frightened until Jesus saved her life and forgave her sin.

> **The thief on the cross,** who said what might have been his first prayer and was promised immediate paradise.

The blind man, who didn't know who Jesus was but only that he himself was blind and now he could see!

The paralyzed boy, whose body needed healing but who first needed to have his sins forgiven.

The prodigal son, who was pretty heartless but who came home when he was hungry into his father's open arms and open heart.

Saul of Tarsus, who was hellbent on destroying Christianity until he took that road to Damascus and found a loving Lord.

God was in Jesus, loving them, affirming them, forgiving them, encouraging them, challenging them all the way into greatness, peace, and the fullness of life: and millions more like them, and like us.

3. The providence of God rules the world. Jesus is the Lord of human history. At times you may experience the feeling that everything is falling apart. You wonder: What is the world coming to? What am I coming to? How will I make ends meet? Who is going to push my wheelchair? You do not consciously define or defend the thought, but sometimes you may be tempted to imagine God with his back to the wall, furious and frustrated at the fact that everything has gotten out of hand. "King Christ, this world is aleak; and lifepreservers there are none" (e. e. cummings). In the words of Saint Paul: "Jesus is the Lord!" You must remember that this world, the course of human history and human destiny are in his hands. He is in charge of this world. He alone has the game plan, total knowledge of the human situation and the power to turn

things around completely. Do not try to make yourself the
Messiah to all people or caretaker to the world. You are
not equipped to cover so much territory or bear such a
burden. Reflect upon these words until they have formed
a new insight in you and have become deeply embedded
in your vision:

> Then Jesus said to his disciples, "That is why I am
> telling you not to worry about your life and what you
> are to eat, not about your body and how you are to
> clothe it. For life means more than food, and the body
> more than clothing. Consider the birds of the air.
> They do not sow or reap; they have no storehouses
> and no barns; yet God feeds them. And how much
> more are you worth than the birds! Can any of you,
> for all his worrying, add a single cubit to his span of
> life? If the smallest things, therefore, are outside your
> control, why worry about the rest? Think of the flow-
> ers; they never have to spin or weave; yet I assure
> you, not even Solomon in all his regalia was robed like
> one of these. Now if that is how God clothes the grass
> in the field which is there today and thrown into the
> furnace tomorrow, how much more will he look after
> you, you of little faith! But you, you must not set your
> hearts on things to eat and things to drink; nor must
> you worry. It is the pagans of this world who set their
> hearts on all these things. Your father well knows you
> need them. No; set your hearts on his kingdom, and
> these other things will be given to you as well."
>
> **Luke 12:22-31**

4. *You are called to love: your God, your self, and
your neighbor.*   God, who is love, has made you in his
image and likeness. Love is your calling and destiny. It is

the perfection of your human nature. Love is also a gift of God, the highest gift of God's Spirit. It is necessary that you realize the importance of loving yourself. There has to be some kind of logical, if not chronological, priority to loving yourself. If you do not love yourself, you will be filled with pain, and this pain will keep all your attention riveted on yourself. Agony constricts our consciousness. If you do not love yourself, you cannot truly love either God or your neighbor. So you must learn to do the same things for yourself that you would do in loving others: You must acknowledge and affirm all that is good in you. You must gently try to understand all that is weak and limited. You must be aware of and try to fulfill your needs: physical, psychological, and spiritual. As you learn to love yourself, you must also learn to balance concern for yourself with concern for others. "Whatever you do for the least of my brothers and sisters you do for me." But remember that your success in loving will be proportionate to your openness in accepting the love and affirmation of God. It will likewise be proportionate to the love that you have for yourself. In the end, the success of your life will be judged by how sensitively and delicately you have loved.

5. *I will be with you.* God says: I am covenanted, committed forever to love you, to do whatever is best for you. I will be kind, encouraging and enabling, but I will also be challenging. At times I will come to comfort you in your affliction. At other times I will come to afflict you in your comfort. Whatever I do, it will always be an act of love and an invitation to growth. I will be with you to illuminate your darkness, to strengthen your weakness, to fill your emptiness, to heal your brokenness, to cure your sickness, to straighten what may be bent in you, and to revive whatever good things may have died in you. Remain united to me, accept my love, enjoy the warmth of my friendship, avail yourself of my power, and you will bear much fruit. You will have life in all its fullness.

6. *Your destiny is eternal life.* God says: By all means join the dance and sing the songs of a full life. At the same time, remember that you are a pilgrim. You are on your way to an eternal home which I have prepared for you. Eternal life has already begun in you but it is not perfectly completed. There are still inevitable sufferings. But remember that the sufferings of this present stage of your life are nothing compared to the glory that you will see revealed in you someday. Eye has not ever seen, nor ear ever heard, nor has the mind ever imagined the joy prepared for you because you have opened yourself to the gift of my love. On your way to our eternal home, enjoy the journey. Let your happiness be double, in the joyful possession of what you have and in the eager anticipation of what will be. Say a resounding "Yes!" to life and to love at all times. Someday you will come up into my mountain, and then for you all the clocks and calendars will have finished their counting. Together with all my children, you will be mine and I will be yours forever.

*   *   *

This is, as I see it, the basic vision proposed in the Gospels (the good news) of Christians. It offers a perspective of life and death—a vision of reality—that is reassuring and at the same time challenging. It provides a needed sense of security, but also meaning and purpose in life. It gives us a basic frame of reference to understand ourselves, our brothers and sisters in the human family, the meaning of life and the world, and God as our loving Father. For the believer it offers a vision of reality or belief system through which all the activating events of our human lives can be interpreted and evaluated. It is a reassurance of what reality is by the Maker of all that is.

This vision of religious faith remains for some people a sweet but mere construct, only a pair of lovely rose-colored glasses to tint and tone down the harsh demands of reality. Again, the decisive factor is personal religious experience, the touch of God. One must be actively engaged with and educated by the Holy Spirit, who alone can make a person a believer. Faith is not a matter of logical reasoning or a natural acquisition. It is a matter of experience. Only God's Spirit can provide the needed religious experience. Only the touch of grace can make the Christian message more than a code of conduct and comfort for pious and plastic people.

It cannot be repeated too often that a living faith is not a human skill or acquisition. We do not pick up "believing" as we would learn, for example, to play the piano. We must be touched by the Spirit of God. The difference in one who has been touched in this way is so profound that Saint Paul calls this person a "new creation." Such a one is, as we say, a new person. Paul calls a life which has not been touched and transformed by the Spirit "life according to the flesh." The life of a person who has been renewed by the Spirit lives a "life according to the Spirit."

Jesus says that it is the Spirit who gives us a certain instinct or intuition that we are affirmed by God. It is through the Spirit that we know we are his beloved children. It is the Spirit who calls out of our hearts the tender and loving words: "Father!"

Even if we did once know Christ in the flesh, that is
not how we know him now. And for everyone who
is in Christ, there is a new creation; the old creation
has gone, and now the new one is here. It is all God's
work. It was God who reconciled us to himself
through Christ and gave us the work of handing on
this reconciliation. In other words, God in Christ was
reconciling the world to himself.

2 Corinthians 5:16-19

Paul himself is so deeply moved by the reality of this
complete transformation that he expresses his personal
experience in the line: "I live, now no longer I, but Christ
lives in me!" (Galatians 2:20).

We have said that we need a vision when we look out
at reality through the eyes of our mind. When we perceive
ourselves, other people, life, the world, and God, we have
to make some kind of an interpretation or evaluation. We
need some kind of order and predictability because we
cannot abide chaos. It is the touch of the Spirit that provides
the kind of focus and clarity that we need in order to see
clearly and to live fully.

In the first words of the first book of the Bible, Genesis,
the Spirit of God is depicted as bringing the order of creation out of the primordial chaos.

In the beginning God created the heavens and the
earth. Now the earth was a formless void [chaos];
there was darkness over the deep, and God's spirit
hovered over the water.

Genesis 1:1-2

It is by this Spirit that confusion and chaos are transformed into the loveliness of creation. Eight chapters later,

in the narration of the Flood, it is the same Spirit of God that causes the waters of the flood to subside. Again he restores the order of creation out of the watery confusion and chaos. Through the prophet Joel, God promises that "it will come to pass that I will pour out my Spirit upon all humankind" (Joel 3:1; quoted in Acts 2:17).

It is this same Spirit of God who comes on the day of Pentecost to transform the disciples of Jesus from cowardly and confused men into clear-headed and convinced apostles. The chaos of their confusion is replaced by great clarity of purpose. It is the Spirit of God who directs the Christians of the early Church. His action appoints leaders, heals the sick, melts hearts, and enables people to love one another in an overwhelming release of power that will renew the face of the earth.

This touch of the Spirit transforms everything in a person and in his or her world. The person is indeed a new creation. The revelation of God, which might otherwise seem to be a fiction, is clearly a fact: a vision of reality. The touch of the Spirit results in a deep harmony, peace and order, replacing a kind of primordial chaos in a human being's inner vision of reality. Consequently, all the emotional and behavioral patterns of the person touched by the Spirit are deeply affected. There is a new sense of integration and wholeness. The person experiences that "unity which has the Spirit as its foundation and peace as its binding force" (Ephesians 4:3). As a new creation, this man or woman is enabled by the Spirit to walk into the beautiful world of God and into the fullness of the life to which God has called his children.

God's Grandeur

The world is charged with the grandeur of God.
It will flame out, like shining from shook foil;
It gathers to a greatness, like the ooze of oil
Crushed. Why do men then now not reck his rod?
Generations have trod, have trod, have trod;
And all is seared with trade; bleared,
    smeared with toil;
And wears man's smudge and shares
    man's smell: the soil
Is bare now, nor can foot feel, being shod.

And for all this, nature is never spent;
There lives the dearest freshness deep down things;
And though the last lights off the black West went
Oh, morning, at the brown brink eastward, springs—
Because the Holy Ghost over the bent
World broods with warm breast and with
    ah! bright wings.

Gerard Manley Hopkins, S.J.

Acknowledgments   *Continued from page ii*

Quotation of Rudolf Dreikurs reprinted with permission of
Macmillan Publishing Co. Inc., from *Contemporary Psychotherapies,*
edited by Morris I. Stein. Copyright © 1961 by The Free Press of
Glencoe, Inc.

From "Sex and Society," by Margaret Mead. Reprinted by
permission of *The Catechist.*

From *Revolt of the Masses,* by José Ortega y Gasset. Copyright 1932
by W. W. Norton & Company, Inc., copyright renewed 1960 by
Teresa Carey.

From *Jesus and Logotherapy,* by Robert Leslie. Copyright © 1965
by Abingdon Press.

From "The No Cop-out Therapy," by Albert Ellis. Copyright
© 1973 by Ziff-Davis Publishing Company. REPRINTED BY
PERMISSION OF PSYCHOLOGY TODAY MAGAZINE.

From *A Few Buttons Missing: The Case Book of a Psychiatrist,* by
James T. Fisher and Lowell S. Hawley. Copyright © 1951 by J. B.
Lippincott. Reprinted by permission of J. B. Lippincott Company.

From "God's Grandeur," by Gerard Manley Hopkins. *Poems of
Gerard Manley Hopkins.* Copyright © 1970 by Oxford
University Press.

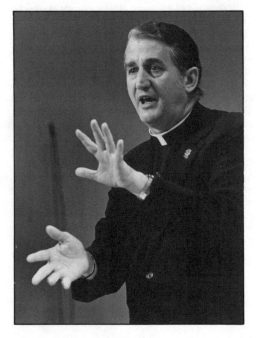

The Fully Alive Experience by John Powell, S.J., and Loretta Brady is a unique program to help you (1) clarify and evaluate life goals and values, (2) explore pathways to a closer relationship with God, and (3) develop a deeply human and Christian life.

This program includes a practical combination of input talks by John Powell and personal exercises by Loretta Brady. The complete program can be implemented by large or small groups in ten two-hour sessions.

The complete kit (#25318) includes:
• 11 Audiocassettes
• 1 Guidebook
• 1 Personal Notebook

The kit, as well as additional Personal Notebooks in packs of ten (#25335), is available from Tabor Publishing, 200 East Bethany Drive, Allen, Texas 75002-3804.